The
Western Isles

Crossing the Minch

The
Western Isles

Francis Thompson

with photographs by
Sam Maynard and Murdo MacLeod

B.T. BATSFORD · LONDON

ISBN 0 7134 5502 0

Typeset by Servis Filmsetting Ltd, Manchester
and printed by Butler & Tanner Ltd
Frome, Somerset
for the Publisher
B.T. Batsford
4 Fitzhardinge Street
London
WIH OAH

Contents

Acknowledgements

The Western Isles have been described as a community of lively people. This they certainly are, having to face up to the many changes, heralding both opportunity and difficulty, which have occurred in the last handful of years. I have to thank both Ian MacIver and Bob Ballard for the germ of the idea which eventually came to reality in this book, and for the chance to write about the islands in these times of change. Thanks too to Murdo MacLeod and Sam Maynard, for their novel approaches to photographing the islands and their folk; to Sharon McNaughton, for transforming my untidy drafts into perfectly typed copy; to the staff of Comhairle nan Eilean for providing a wealth of information about the islands, to say nothing of their hopes for the future; to my wife, Meg, for enduring stoically many lonely evenings while this book was being written.

Taing dhuibhse uile.

Francis Thompson
Stornoway

1. An oceanic setting

The Outer Hebrides, sometimes known as the Western Isles, comprise one of three major groupings of islands off the northern and western shores of Scotland. Lying to the north-west of the Scottish mainland, the islands form a long chain which extends for more than 130 miles from the Butt of Lewis to Barra Head. There are five principal islands: Lewis, which is joined to Harris, North Uist, Benbecula, South Uist and Barra. There are numerous lesser islands, such as Scalpay, Eriskay and Vatersay, all of which support modest but significant populations. There are, however, a number of small islands which once maintained a population. These are now deserted: silent witnesses to the process of desertion in the last century or so when economic and social conditions created problems to which there was only one answer: emigration.

The fact that the Minch and the Sea of the Hebrides have been as effective a barrier as the English Channel has meant that, apart from the aspect of isolation, the folk of the Hebrides have been able to keep intact their unique cultural heritage. This is based on the Gaelic language, one of the five extant sister Celtic indigenous tongues of the British Isles (Welsh, Irish, Manx and Cornish are the other four), which, though now much declined, is still a language of hearth and home and is today witnessing something of a revival. The oceanic perspective of the Western Isles has tended to mould the character of the islanders. Particularly in the southern isles, it is the seascape which dominates the eye; the sea tends to give a particular brightness to daylight, even on those summer days when brooding storm clouds move in from the south-west to bring warm rain with the tangy taste of salt.

All the islands are solidly based on the oldest rock formation in Britain: Lewisian gneiss, a hard unyielding material which has defied millenia of weathering. The rocks were originally igneous and sedimentary in character but have undergone, in an ancient past, several periods of mountain building, which can still be traced in the south-west of Lewis and in Harris. Indeed, the continual exposure of the rocks to sun, wind and rain has prevented vegetation from gaining any kind of hold. Thus, in Harris, one can see vast tables of bare stone which will never carry even a

Sky and sea . . . Uig in Lewis (over)

7

thin scraping of soil for plants. However, that old man of the forest, lichen, manages to make an environment for itself; an age-old survivor clinging to an equally long-lived host.

All the islands have been intensely glaciated. Massive burdens of slow-moving glaciers have worn down much of the sharply serrated land surface to a low undulating platform of rocky knolls and hillocks separated by hollows. Today the rocks bear the imprint of at least two glaciations, with striae or scratchings and deep scoring and gouging where boulders carried in the ice moved against the land surface. In general, the eastern coasts of the islands drop sharply into the waters of the Minch, while, on the western side, the platform slopes gently into the deepening waters of the Atlantic. This sloping has produced a fragmented coastline alleviated by large stretches of sandy beaches. It is thought, too, that a depression or land-sinking in glacial times has contributed to the general east-west tilt of the land base.

Evidence of this depression has been found in the past by fishermen who have dredged up from far below the present high-water line stumps of trees and buried submarine peat, all representing the remains of former vegetation. In the latter years of the sixteenth century, Martin Martin, a visitor from Skye, toured round the Hebrides and published in 1695 the very first popular description of the islands. When he visited Berneray, one of the small islands in the Sound of Harris, he observed: 'The west end of this island which looks to St Kilda, is called the wooden harbour, because the sands at low water discover several trees that have formerly grown there. Sir Norman Macleod told me that he had seen a tree cut there, which was afterwards made into a harrow.'

While the eastern side of the island chain is poor in soil and deficient in sediment, the western coasts present a different story. An abundance of material of organic and mixed organic (shell) origin has created what are called machairs. These are strips of land, hugging the western coast, which are made from shell-bearing sand, accumulated over many centuries to provide extremely fertile soils. Some of these machairs are up to a mile wide and are continually under the influence of the wind, which produces deep corridor blowouts. In general, however, these sand-based lands are fairly stable, helped in no small degree by a cover of vegetation, among which marram and lime grass are the most important. The anchoring effect of these grasses has aided smaller plants to maintain a good foothold and thus offer fine grazing for sheep and cattle. Indeed, the continuous grazing has been a major factor in the formation of the machair. Only when the vegetation has been over-grazed has deterioration of the cover been disturbed, leading to inevitable erosion by wind.

Were it not for these fertile strips of land, the Western Isles would be a poor place in which to live, so dominated is the land by sour, acidic peat.

But for some 3000 years the machair has been farmed in such a way that there has been little loss to either its fertility or its geomorphic interest. In particular, the annual leavening of seaweed as fertilizer has done much to preserve this saving grace. Even today, crofters prefer natural fertilizers to chemicals, which are thought to have a harmful effect on the vegetation and make the machair more susceptible to erosion.

It is a different story when one considers the 'blacklands', the acid soil and peat which overlays much of the islands with an infertile blanket useful only for fuel. Peat consists of decomposed organic matter with a high acid content which checks the bacterial action necessary for good soil to be made. Before the advent of a period of cool wet weather some 3000 years ago, the islands were covered by birch scrub, which developed into birch-pine forest. Tree species included ash, alder, oak and rowan and their remains are still found occasionally in peat bogs cut for fuel. The wet conditions were ideal for the formation of blanket bog and the subsequent accumulation of peat. The trees failed and fell; but even when the Vikings started their raids down the west coast of Scotland around AD 800 there were sufficient stands of woodland – enough at any rate to claim their attention. As one Norse saga puts it: 'Fire played in the fig-trees of Lewis.' When Martin Martin visited Lewis he was moved to write: 'I saw big roots of trees at the head of Loch Erisort, and there is about a hundred young birch and hazel trees on the southwest side of Loch Stornoway, but there is no more wood on the island.'

As the peat bogs thickened the landscape, colours changed to dull greens and browns. An indication of how the peat developed was demonstrated in 1857 when the proprietor of Lewis, Sir James Matheson, decided to excavate what was thought to be some large boulders at Callanish on the west side of Lewis. A depth of five feet of peat was removed to reveal a magnificent megalithic circle, erected around 2000 years BC and evidence of a sophisticated island population having existed at that date. The removal of peat for fuel over the centuries has also exposed boulder clay, glacially deposited on the gneiss rock. This 'skinned ground' or 'gearraidh' forms the basis of a soil which, when mixed with shell-sand and seaweed, becomes quite fertile. It is this land which provides the basis for the form of land use, unique in the British Isles, called crofting. In one respect it offers subsistence income from various agricultural practices, mainly sheep rearing; in another respect crofting has had a social and cultural importance far beyond any other kind of land use – a subject discussed more fully elsewhere in this book.

Lest it might be thought that the Western Isles are storm-bound, rock-based peat bogs, with barren landscapes dotted with small crofting communities huddled together for comfort, it is essential to emphasize that the reality is quite different. To begin with the machairs; this land is a delight to the eye in spring and summer seasons, when the vegetation is a mass of multi-coloured wild flowers, equal to the challenge that any

Persian carpet might offer. The large expanses of silver sand, built up from the shells of long-departed crustacean animals, offer long, lazy and relaxing days in high summer with no overcrowding. Even the moors orchestrate changes in colours as the year progresses. Dark loch waters are dotted with ripples, like some ancient ring-carved stone, as hungry trout rise to take flies. Rivers, particularly after heavy rain, are brown and foam-flecked as they tumble to the sea, offering in their season, the perfect conditions for Atlantic salmon to swim up to their spawning grounds.

And trees there are to be found, with the greatest concentration in Stornoway, in the extensive policies of the Lews Castle. When the castle was built in the 1850s of last century, the wife of the owner, Lady Matheson, decided to create a garden. A vast amount of effort went into creating the right conditions for the plantation, with soil being brought in from the Scottish mainland to supplement the scanty slippering of peaty soil which overlay the hard Lewis rock. Today – while the plantation hardly rivals that of the gardens at Inverewe, in Wester Ross, just across the Minch – the policies support many rare species of trees, including some found only in tropical belts. Rhododendrons, formerly natives of the Himalayas, thrive in Lewis and – in the flowering season, May to July – present a blazing sea of purple and dark green. The reason why tropical species grow in these oceanic islands is the warmth derived from the Gulf Stream, which makes for mild winters. Even palm trees can be seen in a Stornoway garden on Matheson Road! In other parts of the Western Isles there are the welcome sights of smaller plantations, which add some relief to the horizon. Most of these woods have been planted during the last century or so. Natural tree growth is generally difficult in the islands, partly because of the peaty soil and partly because of the strong and frequent winds which make for rather stunted growth.

Afforestation activities have been undertaken on Lewis by the Forestry Commission with two major plantations, both still young and slow growing. Interest in trees as shelter belts for crofts has increased in recent years, but has yet to be put into practice. A lead in experimentation is, however, being undertaken at present by the Stornoway Trust, the body which manages the Lews Castle estate woodlands on behalf of the people of Stornoway, who accepted the policies as a free gift from Lord Leverhulme in 1923.

With the formation of the landscape by glaciers and then the growth of peat, the situation was created for inland water. Lochs abound in the Western Isles. Indeed, one parish in Lewis is actually called Lochs. North Uist, in particular, when viewed from above is studded with lochs, so much so that one might say the total area of the island is more fresh water than land. Lewis has well over one thousand patches of fresh water, great

The mechanized cutting of peat produces these pipe-like furrows in the acid soil of the 'blacklands'

and small. Loch Scadavay in North Uist has such an irregular shore line that, though its dimensions are about two miles by four, its perimeter is over fifty miles. Loch Langavat (Norse: Long Water) covers no less than eight separate rock basins. The vast majority of lochs carry stocks of brown trout, most of which are around the 3–4-lb mark, though occasionally much larger fish can be caught. Sea trout and rainbow trout are also found, the latter as the result of re-stocking. The char, a beautifully coloured fish of the salmon family, is found in some Hebridean lochs, including Loch Fada in North Uist. The eel is another familiar species, now the subject of a small commercial enterprise on the west side of Lewis, which hopes to exploit the mainland market for smoked eels.

Most of the rivers in the Western Isles are short-run. Even so, they have attracted the Atlantic salmon for centuries and still do, though nowadays to a lesser extent – the result of the huge catches of the fish by commercial fishing interests, which intercept the fish as they swim towards Scotland's rivers. Many of the rivers in North Uist, Harris and Lewis are well noted by anglers for their salmon. The Grimersta River in Lewis, with its complex loch system, has been called the finest salmon river in Europe. However, the halcyon days of yesteryear, when a day's catch could yield fifty fish, are well and truly gone forever.

Inevitably the maritime nature of the Western Isles has dictated the range of flora and fauna to be found in the islands. And, as inevitably, their separation from the Scottish mainland has produced some sub-species and none at all of those species which might have been expected to survive. For instance, the Outer Hebrides not only lack amphibians but have only one reptile, the slow-worm, which is found in scattered colonies. Red deer, however, are found mainly on the hilly fastnesses; they tend to be on the small side, due to lack of feeding, and are, as might be expected, well poached. Otters love the island rivers, where they feast on trout and salmon. Though widespread, they tend to be nocturnal of habit and rather elusive, though their whistling calls may often be heard on the days of high summer. The mink, an imported species, has become very well established since the 1960s, the result of escaping from farms where they were bred for their fur. In Harris and Lewis, in particular, they have become predators on other species of wild life. The mink is a fierce carnivore, which has not been slow in exploiting whatever food resources it finds in its hunting areas.

While bird life on the moors tends to be sparse, it is found in teeming thousands on the shoresides and cliffs of the islands. Some birds are peculiar to the area, such as the Hebridean sub-species of the twite, dunnock, song-thrush and wren. The woods of the Lews Castle at Stornoway offer a long list of species, resident, wintering and migrant. In

Loch Raoinavat, Shawbost, Lewis

North and South Uist the corncrake has found its final place of safety, having been forced out of its former areas on the British mainland by extensive farming activity.

Of particular importance is the Nature Reserve at Loch Druidibeag in South Uist. Extending to over 4000 acres, this natural environment is largely owned by the Nature Conservancy and contains a wealth of topographical features ranging from lochs with miniature islands, peninsulas, indented shorelines, marshes and machair land. The highlight of the bird life in the area is the gray lag goose which breeds wild hereabouts, though some might prefer the golden eagle, the hen harrier or the red-necked phalarope. Several of the loch's islands, owing to their isolation from fire and grazing, are covered with a relic scrub woodland of birch, rowan, willow, juniper, bramble and wild rose, all of which are echoes of the former glory which once covered much of the Western Isles.

It is, however, the seas round the Western Isles which teem with an abounding richness, though much of this wealth has gone – the inevitable result of over-fishing; some once-valuable fishing banks are now quite barren. As early as the reign of King James V of Scotland, in the sixteenth century, Dutch fishing busses made their appearance here for the rich pickings of prime high-quality fish. In 1594 the Dutch made their first recorded visit to Lewis, operating under a licence which allowed them to fish outside a limit of 28 miles. The success of the Dutch attracted the attention of the Scots and, by the time James VI of Scotland had become James I of England, the Hebridean waters were being fully exploited. James' son, Charles I, was similarly enticed by the Minch and backed proposals for the formation of a new corporation, under English auspices, which would develop the Hebridean fisheries industry. The corporation, founded in 1633, was the 'Company of the General Fishery of Great Britain and Ireland' with its main seat of operation based in Lewis. A number of fishing stations were established in Harris and North Uist, on the island of Hermetray in the Sound of Harris. Martin Martin, writing of this island at the close of the century, says he saw '. . . the foundation of a house, built by the English, in King Charles the First's time, for one of their magazines to lay up the casks, salt, etc, for carrying on the fishery, which was then begun in the Western Isles; but this design miscarried because of the civil wars which then broke out.' The scheme fell flat in 1640 and, though Charles II tried to revive it on a commercial basis, lack of capital caused it again to come to nothing.

But the then owner of Lewis, Lord Seaforth, decided to take matters into his own hands and, in contravention of the laws and privileges of Scottish Royal Burghs, set up Stornoway as a fishing port and imported Dutch fishermen to prosecute the fishing. This lasted until the outbreak

A peregrine falcon is re-released into the wild after treatment for injury by SSPCA Inspector John MacAvoy

of hostilities between Britain and Holland in 1653, when the Dutch nationals had to leave.

From then on the interest in large-scale fishing was spasmodic, though the export of good quality fish continued. It was not until the middle of last century that the potential in the fishing grounds in the Minch waters was fully realised. Herring was the main attraction, and it was not long before Castlebay in Barra, Lochboisdale in South Uist, Lochmaddy in North Uist and Stornoway in Lewis became major fishing ports, servicing literally thousands of fishing boats – mainly from the east coast of Scotland. At one time, in fact, Stornoway was one of the world's major herring ports. The herring fishing declined soon after World War I – and has declined ever since until now, to conserve the species, closed seasons are regularly announced.

The advent of the steam trawler at the turn of the century, and – in later years – the new methods of catching young to mature fish, heralded the beginning of the end. Now local boats can spend a day scouring the Minch for white fish and return with nothing. On the west coast of the Western Isles, however, prime fish in commercial quantities exist and no doubt, in time, these too will disappear. Even sand eels, these small fish which are the main food resource of other species, are being swept up in their thousands of tons for fish meal. Conservation has yet to be accepted by fishermen.

Conservation of species, as a generally accepted policy for the protection of the future, is as much an issue on land as it is at sea. In recent years, many parts of the Western Isles have been declared by the Nature Conservancy as being of particular importance to various kinds of wild life. The problem is that people also have to live off the land. In general, the crofting way of life tends to allow for land management techniques which do little to harm wild life. But the need for new land, reclaimed from peat bogs, is ever pressing and the techniques involved inevitably disturb existing havens for birds and plants. Land which through neglect has become waterlogged is prized by wild fowl as breeding grounds. But when the opportunity comes along for a crofter to drain the land, controversy rages over the proposal with the question: Is the protection of birds more important than the protection of the human species, which tries to make a fitful living on whatever land can be reclaimed and put into better use?

While the islands of the Hebrides are interesting enough in themselves, their satellites are equally deserving of attention, though they tend to be remote and difficult of access. Perhaps the best known group of island outliers is St Kilda, deserted by its residual population in 1930, and now under the care of the National Trust for Scotland. It is used as a rocket tracking station by the Army. These activities are well confined so that the main island in the group, Hirt, is kept intact as a kind of living museum to commemmorate a community of islanders who eventually found the

Eriskay from South Uist

pressures of island living so unbearable that they had to ask the Government for assistance in their removal. Indeed, St Kilda tends to be a lesson for all who live on small islands; the time comes when the residents must ask what minimum standard of life and living is required to keep their community buoyant and stable. The problem always rests with the ambitions of the young folk, who, as ever, pull on the traces and yearn for the life as portrayed on television screens. And, as all remote communities are aware, when the young leave, there is nothing left but eventual desertion of the home and hearth, as the older generation fades away.

Even in the Western Isles, islands have been deserted in living memory. Scarp, off the west coast of Harris, was deserted within the last decade or so. Vatersay, off Barra, is in a similar situation, where basic services, such as medical attention, are not at immediate hand. Other small island communities tend to have a direct means of communication with their mainland landmass, which helps to ease the mind of problems. Other islands, like Eriskay and Scalpay, depend on ferries, but are fortunate in having communities which are proudly independent and are able to work out their own salvation. In fact, these two island communities have developed strong economies based on fishing.

It should be emphasized that the entire population of the Western Isles is slightly over 30,000, no more than one would expect in a large town on the British mainland. Just over 75 per cent live in Lewis and Harris; 20 per cent in the Uists and Benbecula and 5 per cent in Barra. Stornoway and its immediate environs, with a population of 8100 persons, is by far the largest concentration of the population. In fact, more people live in Stornoway than in the whole of the southern Isles. The four off-shore islands which still support a population, Scalpay, Eriskay, Berneray and Vatersay, account for about 900 people. Thus, as in Scotland's other island groups, like Orkney, with a population of less than 20,000 people, the future, one might suggest, is not all that certain, particularly when one considers that the employment situation for young people is not one filled with bright hope.

While there has always been a definite attraction to island living, there is also the keen edge of reality to be considered. Not being self-sufficient, the Western Isles depend overmuch on what the ferries bring across the waters to Castlebay, Lochmaddy and Stornoway. This dependence on the Scottish mainland has occasionally been highlighted when seamen take strike action. On the other hand, these occasions have demonstrated that the islanders possess enough initiative to overcome the problems which these actions create. That being said, there still remains among the islefolk a strong sense of belonging. 'Home' is not necessarily a house; rather it is the township or island where one was born and brought up. In summer expatriate islanders flock to their native heaths and hearths, favouring the islands to the brash and brazen attractions of the Costa del Sol and similar venues for holidays.

The Western Isles have been identified as an area of important natural and built environment (including historic and archaeological remains). Indeed, the combination of land, sea and inland water in the islands has produced landscapes of outstanding, and even international importance. In terms of flora and fauna the islands possess a high significance. If the British corncrake has had to resort to the Western Isles to seek solace, what other species might eventually turn northwards for their very survival into the future? Yet the future is also uncertain for the human population. Can one be sure that the islands of Vatersay (pop: 107) and Berneray (pop: 132) will still maintain their present communities of lively people a century hence? It is this thought that visitors to these islands must bear in mind as they journey through. Indeed, it is a thought that the islanders themselves must contend with on a daily basis, for it is those more mature members of island society who must endeavour to create the right conditions for the rising younger generation, so that the Western Isles in the future is not one vast conservation area, rich in wild life but devoid of people.

Tarbert, with The Hebrides *coming into the roll-on roll-off pier*

2. Prehistory

While the Western Isles cannot claim to possess the same store of rich archaeological sites as, say, Orkney, the islands are in fact well up on the list, with much visible evidence of a continuous history of occupation by the human species going back many thousands of years. Excavation work in recent years has revealed new finds of significance, and no doubt similar work in the future will expose further proof that the islands offered to primitive peoples a good environment in which to live and work.

The first people similar to modern man first began to appear in Europe around 30,000 years ago. Their progress across the continent was slow and gradual. So far as Scotland is concerned, colonies of hunter/gatherers appeared around 10,000 BC during what is called the Neolithic period, the New Stone Age. Evidence of the presence of these people has been found in an area near Callanish on the west side of Lewis, where woodland was cleared for growing crops, in the form of a pollen record. The presence of charcoal suggests that a policy of deliberate burning of woodland occurred around 5000 BC. It is generally accepted that the islands were inhabited by a settled resident Mesolithic community at this time.

The building of megalithic or great-stone tombs began between 3000 and 2000 BC, representing the Neolithic period. Indeed, there is more evidence from archaeology of the dead than the living. The reason for this is that domestic buildings were more often of wood than stone. Wood deteriorates above ground and only post holes below ground level give clues as to the location of settlements. What yet lies beneath the Hebridean peat may well surprise future archaeologists.

Occasionally, Neolithic houses are revealed by coastal erosion. Excavation at Udal, North Uist, and Northton, Harris, has revealed ancient settlements. But these two sites are far outnumbered by the 30 or so megalithic tombs to be found in the Western Isles. The tombs are of two basic types, though there are many variants. 'Passage grave' is the name given to those which consist of a chamber entered by a passageway and set within a circular cairn, the edge of which is defined by a kerb of large stones. About two thirds of the chambered tombs in the Western Isles are to be found in North Uist. Four of these have long cairns and fifteen are of the circular cairn type. Two sites of interest are Barba nam

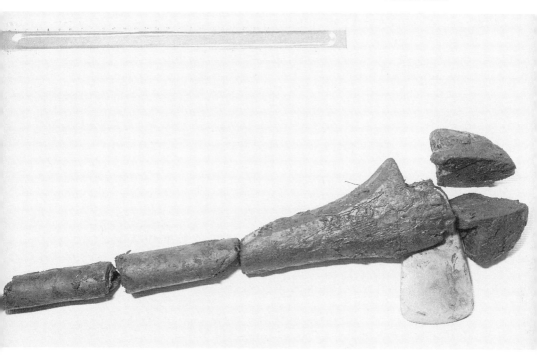

A stone-age axe found buried in a peat bank at Point in April 1982

Feannag, North Uist, and at Airidh na h-aon Oidhche, South Uist, which is more accessible.

There is evidence to suggest that these tombs were used regularly over a period of centuries before they were finally closed up. The number of tombs, and their scattered location indicates that they may have had a tribal significance, and that they were much more than simple tombs. Thus the picture builds up of the Western Isles supporting a number of self-contained communities, each with its own identifiable territory and with the tomb acting as a focal point for occasions of communal significance, like the market cross in later times.

The Neolithic period ended around 2000 BC with the introduction of metalworking settlers and the beginning of what is called the Bronze Age. This period was heralded by a change in climatic conditions, with the Western Isles in particular becoming much wetter and colder, heralding the beginning of the formation of the peat bogs. The resident population moved from inland areas to the coastal strips as the peat spread from hitherto arable land. And, not surprisingly, the peat, which not only changed the landscape, also began to swallow up the monuments of the Bronze Age. The larger sites are still visible above the peat, but of farms,

View from Carloway (Lewis), looking south towards Great Bernera (over)

settlements and other low-level buildings no trace can be seen.

It was during the Bronze Age that the building of stone circles became a particular activity of these ancient peoples. Over 20 such circles have been identified in the Western Isles, with one, at Achmore in Lewis, being discovered and excavated only a handful of years ago. The most perfect example is to be found at Callanish, again in Lewis, which is only one of a group of sites located around Loch Roag. The Callanish Circle is second only to Stonehenge in importance among the stone circles in Britain. Like the chambered tombs, the circles contain burial chambers, but there are a number of suggestions as to their specific purpose apart from being memorials to the dead. Strong arguments have been put forward to the effect that the circles are astronomical observatories. Certainly their geometry is complex, but whether this was achieved by accident or design is a matter for raging controversy. So far as the non-professional visitor is concerned, it is sufficient to stand back and admire these stones and wonder at the nature of the communities who erected them.

To list all the sites in the Western Isles would be tedious, but the following are reasonably accessible and well worth a visit.

GARRABOST, Lewis (NB 523 330): A chambered cairn almost totally destroyed, but with seven of its kerb stones still standing. A number of stones can be seen which were more than likely part of the central chamber.

COLL, Lewis (NB 450 382): This cairn is in poor condition, as a result, no doubt, of raiding in recent times for building material. The remains of a circular chamber are visible, as are a few large slabs lying in the chamber which may have formed part of a corbelled roofing.

GRESS, Lewis (NB 472 438): This chambered cairn is unusual in that it seems to have been erected on a platform which is partially man-made. Part of the usual kerb feature is visible around the south-western side.

BALLANTRUSHAL, Lewis (NB 375 537): This is the Clach an Trushal, a magnificent monolith standing about 19 ft high. Lewis tradition associates the stone with the commemoration of a battle between two island clans, but the stone pre-dates any such incident in recorded history. In Gaelic, the name has a 'sorrowful' connotation, so there may well be a glimmer of truth in the legend – but dating much later than the stone itself.

CALLANISH, Lewis (NB 213 330): This, of course, is the most spectacular of all circles in the Western Isles. It consists of a small chambered tomb set within a stone circle from which a series of lines of stone radiate towards the cardinal points of the compass. Fragments of human bone were recovered from the chamber when excavation work was carried out in 1857, when some five feet of peat deposit were removed. Lewis tradition has it that certain families in the locality were 'keepers' of the stones, which were used in historical times for ceremonies of an uncertain nature. Recent excavations have indicated that the geometry of the site is complex and there is evidence for its alignment with other stone sites in the far distance.

GARYNAHINE, Lewis (NB 230 303): This is one of three sites lying within a half mile of each other. Located on the northern slope of a low hill it commands excellent views in all directions, except southwards. The other two sites are at NB 225 335 and NB 222 335.

BARPA LANGASS, North Uist (NF 837 656): This is a passage grave easily accessible and is probably the best preserved of all the chambered tombs on the island. It is possible to gain entry into the chamber, though a torch is needed. In 1911 finds included Neolithic pottery, flint objects and Bronze Age beaker pottery.

POBULL FHINN, North Uist (NF 843 651): This stone circle is roughly oval in shape and sits on a platform which might have been manmade. A total of 24 stones and boulders can be seen, averaging about a metre in height.

CROANAVAL, North Uist (NF 830 630): This site is interesting because of the number of monuments in the immediate locality. These include two large stone slabs, three small cairns, and a simple stone circle.

CARINISH, North Uist (NF 833 602): This would have been a fine stone circle were it not for the fact that the A865 road cuts through it and had further insult been added to injury by recent road widening activity. Now only shattered stumps of stone remain.

CLETTRAVAL, North Uist (NF 749 713): This site has a long chambered cairn and an Iron Age wheelhouse. The cairn was originally wedge-shaped, with its western end partially dismantled to construct the wheelhouse, so called because the chambers radiate from a central point. The site excavations revealed a mass of Neolithic and Beaker pottery which are now housed in the National Museum of Antiquities in Edinburgh.

AIRIDH NA H-AON OIDHCHE, Benbecula (NF 817 525): A chambered long cairn which has yet to be properly excavated to reveal its true nature.

KILPHEDAR, South Uist (NF 735 205): This is an excellent example of a wheelhouse or aisled house. Situated on the machair it suffers from frequent sand blows. It consists of a circular house dug into the sand. Eleven stone piers are set radially to the wall but do not touch it, thus providing an 'aisle'.

Interesting though these reminders of an ancient Hebridean people might be, there are others which are of more recent date: the brochs and duns.

These structures are peculiar to northern Scotland and belong to the Iron Age between roughly 300 BC to AD 300. They were fortified towers, circular and beehive in shape, with thick walls in which stairs and chambers were located. When the Norse first saw them they assumed them to be defensive structures. From the number of these structures found in Orkney, around 100, it is thought that broch-building began there and spread throughout the north of Scotland. The most perfect example is Mousa Broch in Shetland, with the structure at Dun Carloway, in Lewis, ranking second in its size, complexity and state of preservation. Two other very good examples are to be found in Glenelg, in the Scottish mainland parish which fronts on to the Sound of Sleat, in Skye. It is thought that their function was to afford the nearby community some degree of safety when raiders appeared on the scene. Men, women and children would be herded into the broch, possibly with some of the domestic animals, while the marauders focussed their attention on the dwellings outside.

The Western Isles are not so well endowed with these structures as are other places. There are only 14 sites compared with 28 on Skye. Both North and South Uist have two sites, while Benbecula has none.

Far more numerous, though they are on a smaller scale, are the duns, of which there are the remains of some 120 in the Hebrides. These are basically fortified sites, usually with a roughly circular wall constructed of rough stone. An excavation at Dun Cuier, on Barra, revealed bone combs and a mould for making glass beads, suggesting a date for its occupation around AD 600. Being smaller than the brochs they may well have been used by one or two families rather than a large community.

In addition to these structures there are promontory forts dating from the Iron Age period. Basically they consist of a thick wall of stone covering the neck of a promontory, to afford some protection against the enemy. The fort near Barra Head lighthouse actually has a galleried stone wall built across the promontory to defend the landward side, with the 600 ft high cliffs on the seaward side affording more than adequate protection. Again the following list is not exhaustive, but includes those sites reasonably accessible.

LOWER BAYBLE, Lewis (NB 516 305): This dun is in Loch an Dun and is in a rather ruinous state, though part of the outer wall can be seen, as can the stone causeway leading from the lochside to the dun itself.

RUBHA NA BEIGHRE, Lewis (NB 235 474): This is a promontory fort built on a sea-girt rock and joined to the land by a narrow neck across which a massive stone wall has been erected. Though now quite tumbled down, the amount of stone lying around suggests the wall presented an almost impassable obstruction to the enemy.

DUN CARLOWAY, Lewis (NB 189 412): This is the broch which is on every visitor's 'must' list. Even allowing for the fact that it is rather incomplete, its siting is quite impressive. The highest part of the double wall is over 27 ft. Entrance to the broch is gained through a low opening which has a guard cell in the south wall of the entrance passage. One can climb up into the galleried wall for a moment of contemplation on the lifestyle of these early islanders.

Dun baravat, Lewis (NB 156 356): This is a galleried dun which is built on a small islet in Loch Baravat on the island of Great Bernera. The north facing wall is well preserved with a height of about 10 ft.

Dun sticer, North Uist (NB 898 778): Approached by a well constructed causeway, the broch has been badly damaged by a rectangular structure dating about the sixteenth century. Local tradition has it that it was a residence of a baillie of Lord Macdonald of Sleat.

Dun torcuill, North Uist (NB 889 738): This is the island's best example of a broch but is so filled with fallen stones that the entrances to the round gallery cannot now be seen.

Dun mor, South Uist (NF 778 415): This is a fortified island approached by a man-made causeway. There is evidence that this site, along with others of the South Uist duns, were refortified and re-used a number of times in the post-medieval period.

Who were these early Hebrideans who left such impressive monuments in stone? Of their domestic and social life there is little solid evidence to indicate how their lives were organized. The number of theories which abound like flakes in a snow flurry regarding such relics as Callanish and Dun Carloway only serve to give each person his say without fear of contradiction from another. But a general picture can be derived from evidence revealed elsewhere in Britain and in Europe.

That in Scotland there is no indication of the Palaeolithic (Old Stone Age) settlers is probably due to the fact that glacial periods have destroyed whatever evidence they might have left. In any case, these people tended to be cave-dwellers dependent for their survival on the herds of bison and other animals which grazed on the tundra at the edge of the ice sheets. As the temperature rose, forests took over to force tribes to diversify their food sources and to rely on vegetables, nuts and fruits, and to become hunter-gatherers. The Middle Stone Age, the Mesolithic, gave way to the Neolithic or New Stone Age, in which farming was the basis of the new economic system. Whether people of this period lived in the Western Isles is a matter for conjecture. Most of the known Scottish sites tend to be found on or near raised beaches, close to the sea. There are, however, no raised beaches in the Western Isles. But as the sea level has risen continuously since the end of the Ice Age, any Mesolithic evidence may well be drowned more than a few miles off-shore. That some sites are found in the Inner Hebrides suggests that the Western Isles were also inhabited during the period. As has been described earlier, the only evidence is found near Tob-an-Leobag, near Callanish.

The Mesolithic people lived in camps which were seasonally occupied, and so located as to take advantage of the available food resources offered throughout the year. Evidence for houses is completely lacking. Most sites are of the type called 'middens', which are, as the name implies, simply refuse heaps of food debris, shells and bones, derived from shellfish, fresh and salt-water fish, and land animals such as the red deer. One, at Hornish Point, South Uist, is now being excavated.

When the New Stone Age people arrived in the Western Isles they came as settlers, bringing their new knowledge and techniques of farming with them. No doubt spreading in from Skye, crossing the Minch waters in skin-covered boats, they mixed and inter-married with the older people they found to create a new basis for communal economy. These Neolithic people also brought other techniques with them, in particular the building of monuments in stone. New ideas and philosophies were also imported to give a significance to the great stone tombs such as that at Barpa Langass on North Uist. The technique of corbelling, in which walls as they rise come closer together and are, finally, capped with a large stone slab, is a deceptively simple method of building, but had yet to be discovered by a people familiar only with the construction of chambers.

Many cairns have their entrances aligned south and east, so that the sun at its rise or setting could shine its rays into the central chamber on certain dates of the year. The recent work by Colin Renfrew suggests that while these cairns acted as graves, they were also markers for a tribal area of agricultural land. Thus a picture is built of a people whose culture was becoming sophisticated. This Neolithic period was probably the equivalent of a Golden Age, with the people enjoying high standards of life and living, with plenty of time available to indulge in the ceremonies of religion, and to erect such monuments as would act as focal points for the communal activities related to the mind rather than the belly.

When the Bronze Age arrived, the people became the 'Beaker Folk', so-called because of the distinctive style of pottery they produced. In this connection there is on Eilean-an-Tighe, a rocky islet in Loch nan Geireann in North Uist, what may prove to be the oldest recorded example in Western Europe of a potter's workshop. So many potsherds and wasters have been found that nothing less than a pottery factory could have existed here – to supply the needs of the inhabitants of the island and those of the neighbouring islands. The pottery is of high quality and the patterns show great variety and artistry. The foundations exposed during excavation revealed a pit and a couple of kilns. Much of the earthenware found on the site of the chambered cairn at Clettraval came from Eilean-an-Tighe.

While the building of chambered cairns is impressive enough, the stone circles represent an equally outstanding achievement of these ancient folk. Again arguments rage as to their purpose and it is not the function of this chapter to accept any or none. Suffice to say that these henges indicate

Professor Dennis Harding of Edinburgh University Archaeological Research Centre supervises a dig at the First-Century Broch at Reef Beach Machair, Uig, Lewis

a further development in the sophistication of the Hebridean people. The existence of Iron Age forts gives another clue as to the pressures placed on Hebridean society, with the need for protection against marauders, from whence they might come. Both brochs and duns indicate the urgent need for places of safety. One can easily imagine fleets of pirate boats using the inter-island waters as highways to plunder, reflecting the similar piratical deeds of one of the Macneills of Barra in a later time.

No doubt by the time of the birth of Christ Hebridean society was well stratified with chiefs, warrior classes, aristocracy and common folk, with special social niches for priests and bards to cater for the needs of the mind and heart. This, in fact, was the kind of society which was to become established in later times with the Highland clans.

We have yet to give a name to these people, in particular those of the late Iron Age, who lived in the Western Isles. Any person who was found north of the Antonine Wall, stretching between the Forth and the Clyde, was called by the Romans a Pict, from Pictii or Painted Ones. This race of people have left hardly anything of their civilization, save some magnificent carved stones and a few placename elements, such as 'pit'. They were widespread in the north of Scotland and it is not so fanciful to imagine that they had a presence in the Hebrides. They were the pre-Celtic people, who were slowly but surely replaced by the Scotii from Ireland who first gained a foothold in Scotland in the Argyll area and spread to as many corners as they could find, to establish small kingdoms. The residual Picts and Scots were eventually amalgamated into the nation of Scotland by Kenneth MacAlpin in 841, a process in which the Picts completely lost their former identity.

It is known that the Picts of the embryo Scotland traded with the Northern Irish Celts. When one compares the carved Pictish stones and the ornamented carved stones of the early Celts there are many parallels in the techniques used in artistic expression. It would follow that in the context of social structure, and the existence of a warrior aristocracy, that there were only subtle differences between the two races. Thus one might assume that from the beginning of the Christian datings the inhabitants of the Western Isles were Picts, though they left in these islands none of the magnificent sculptured stones found in the north-east and eastern parts of Scotland.

The picture then at the dawning of the age of Christianity is the Western Isles suffering from a significant change in climate, with ancient stone-built memorials slowly drowning in a landscape of peat, the folk huddling round the more congenial machair coastlines and prosecuting the means for living as best they could and, no doubt, reflecting on the tales of bygone eras as told by the storytellers on cold winters' nights. If they reflected on the changes which had occurred in the past, their children and future generations were to look forward to equally significant changes which were just round the corner.

3. Historic times

During the first five centuries AD, the Scotii from Ireland who had settled in Argyll, or Dalriada as that ancient kingdom was known, increased their numbers, their power and their influence and began to spread farther afield, slowly if not always too carefully. It was St Columba, however, who gave an impetus to the infiltration of Irish Celts into the more remote parts of the west of Scotland and the islands. His landing on Iona in 563 started a movement which is still remembered in the lore of the folk of the Western Isles. Of royal Irish descent, his influence was both Christian and political, which gave his itinerant missionaries some kind of authority as they took the words of the Gospel to the pagan Picts.

The kind of Christianity introduced by Columba was based on the monastic ideal and centred on monasteries under the control of abbots, in sharp contrast to the contemporary Roman-based religion, which was organized in dioceses and parishes under the control of bishops. Under Columba's organization, bishops were lesser lights under the authority of abbots. There are a number of sites in the Western Isles which echo these early days. The site of Teampull Chaluim Cille (Columba) in Benbecula once consisted of a cashel with a church situated a short distance away. At Howmor in South Uist are a couple of early chapels and at Kilbar on Barra a church and two chapels can be seen. These sites are thought to represent cashels: areas enclosed by a wall or ditch and bank, within which were located churches and small chapels with accommodation for the clerics.

The area thus enclosed was outside the law of the land and so gave sanctuary to fugitives from local justice. Safety was not always guaranteed, however, for many old records tell of men being slain 'in the doorway of the church'. The cashel was also the area in which the material wealth of the religious community was kept, which may well be the reason why they were such attractions for the marauding Vikings who were to appear on the scene by the seventh century AD. The placename elements 'kil', derived ultimately from the Latin cella or church, and Teampull (Latin: templum) are common in the Western Isles and are a reasonably sure sign that the site was once occupied by a simple structure in which a Columban missionary held his services. Many of these sites are also associated with a saint's name, usually that of Columba, but often of one of his followers, as it is not recorded that Columba himself ever visited the Western Isles.

Only Barra derives its name from a saint, from St Barr or Finbarr, who is also the founding saint of the city of Cork in Ireland. Whether Finbarr ever visited the Western Isles is rather doubtful and it may well be that the real founding saint of the island is Barrfhionn, from whom the parish of Kilbarron in the diocese of Raphoe in Ireland takes its name and origin. This saint is probably identical with Barinthus who is said in some of the accounts of the sailor-saint, Brendan, to have inspired the latter's voyages. In fact, St Brendan also receives some recognition in Barra, which is appropriate, as his famous voyage in his leather-built craft took him up the waters of the Minch and on to Iceland and the New World.

Near the Butt of Lewis is another interesting building, a church dedicated to St Moluag and built on the site of a sixth-century chapel by, no doubt, the saint himself who was a companion of St Columba. The present building dates from the twelfth century, being founded by Olav the Black during the Norse occupation of the islands. But there is another interpretation of 'Moluag', in that the prefix 'mo' is an honorific or respectful mode of address with the 'luag' part, being derived from the name of the Celtic and pagan God Luaidh. It was not uncommon for these Celtic gods and goddesses to be Christianized with Bridget, now St Bride, being a favourite dedicatee.

From archaeological excavations and pollen counts there is evidence that the advent of Columban missionaries on the islands led to an increase in arable cultivation by the resident population, thus providing a new factor in the social organization of the islanders.

Other evidence of the Christianizing era is found in the form of simple monuments. While there are very few of the elaborately carved crosses found in many places of ecclesiastical importance throughout Scotland, a small number can be seen in the Hebrides. Slabs bearing simple Latin crosses are found at Clach an Teampull, on the island of Taransay, off the west coast of Harris; at Teampull Mhuire, on Vallay, North Uist; and at Bagh Bhan on Pabbay in the Sound of Harris. These were more than likely used as grave markers. These slabs date from around the seventh century. The slab from Pabbay, now in the National Museum of Antiquities in Edinburgh, is interesting because it bears witness to the Christianizing of the Picts. It shows two Pictish symbols surmounted by a simple incised cross and is displayed in the company of another Pictish carving found in the Western isles at Strome Shunnamul, in Benbecula. These stones tend to add weight to the reckoning that the early folk of the Western Isles were, indeed, Picts.

If the Celtic missionaries from Iona brought with them an era of social wellbeing, and perhaps some peace of both mind and heart, it was not to last, for in Scandinavia the Vikings were beginning to feel a stirring in their bones. These Norse adventurers first directed their attention to the Orkney and Shetland islands and then moved towards Iceland and

Greenland and the Western Isles from the opening years of the ninth century. The Irish Annals tell us that Skye was pillaged by the Vikings in 794 and, no doubt, Lewis and the other islands received similar attention then and previously. One cannot say for certain that they used these islands for settlements or simply seasonal bases. It was not until the end of the ninth century that the oppressive rule of Harold the Fair-haired began the flowing stream of Norse emigration which rapidly colonized Iceland, the Faroes, Orkney and Shetland and the Hebrides. There seems to be no mention of the Hebrides in history until 1014, the year of the Battle of Clontarf in Ireland. In that year, according to an Irish manuscript, foreigners (Scandinavians) from 'Leodus' (Lewis) fought under the banner of Sigurd, Jarl of Orkney, against the native Irish. Under the date 1098 there is an allusion to Lewis in the Icelandic Sagas. That was the year in which Magnus Bareleg (the only Norse king on record who wore the kilt) plundered Lewis and devastated the island with fire and sword.

Other unwelcome visitors included Rolf the Ganger, who founded Normandy in 876, and called in at the Hebrides on his way south. King Eric, who succeeded Harald on his abdication in 930, also visited the Western Isles, as did King Olav who reigned from 968 to 1000. Towards the end of the tenth century Jarl Torfinn Sigurdson took possession of the Hebrides.

The mystery is: where is the evidence of Viking settlements in the islands? There are no Viking villages, no ship graves like the one on the island of Canna, south of Skye. Yet, the placenames give the game away. Of the 126 recognizable village names on Lewis, for instance, 99 are of wholly Scandinavian origin, while a further 11 are partly Scandinavian. From this evidence there can be no doubt that the Viking settlements in the Western Isles were quite extensive. One suggestion is that, once the Viking houses were abandoned, they simply disappeared into the ground – to become indistinguishable from the remains of the numerous 'black houses' of a later date. The typical Viking house was a long rectangular building, divided along its length into three parallel strips. The two outer strips were slightly raised and the beds were located there. The centre strip contained the hearth. Once abandoned, these dwellings decay to leave simple rectangular mounds in which only faint outlines of the outer walls remain visible. But so are the remains of the walls of abandoned black houses. Only proper excavation will yield answers and, as there is no urgency to discover evidence of Viking presence in the Western Isles, we may wait a long time to find out.

Norse rule ended with the Battle of Largs in 1263, when King Haakon Haakonson was forced to accept defeat, and retreated to the northern isles, where he died. Peace was concluded with the Scots by Magnus, Haakon's son, in 1266, when the Hebrides were ceded to King Alexander of Scotland, though it is interesting that the Hebrides, Inner and Outer, continued to be ruled by the dynasty of Somerled, known as the Lords of the Isles. This Somerled married a daughter of King Olaf who was King of the Hebrides from 1113 to 1153.

Apart from placenames, the Norse left other marks on the Western Isles; these are hardly visible, yet their presence is still around today in the form of families and clans. Many clans of the north-west claim a Norse ancestry. Some claim a Gaelic one. But both have in their veins Celtic and Pictish blood. The Clan MacLeod, who are today most numerous in Lewis, Harris and Skye, trace their origins to Liotr, a younger son of Olav the Black, King of Man and the Northern Isles. The Morrisons of Lewis claim descent from Somerled, already mentioned. They became hereditary judges, or breves, and exercised significant power, not always in the interest of the island. The MacAulays, most numerous in Uig, Lewis, were the forebears of Lord MacAulay, the eminent English historian and essayist. Other Lewis families include MacIvers, MacRaes and Nicolsons. In the Uists, MacDonalds were numerous, derived from the fact that these islands came under the jurisdiction of the Lordship of the Isles. On Barra, the MacNeils came to power as the result of a granting to them of the overlordship of that island by Norse kings. Later, they had their title confirmed by a Charter granted in 1427 by the Lords of the Isles. After the Lordship of the Isles was dissolved, the charter to the MacNeils was again confirmed by King James IV in 1495.

The MacNeils inherited much of their Norse associations; they were excellent seamen and indulged in piracy. Many were the times the inhabitants of the coasts of Northern Ireland looked seaward to see MacNeil's longships scudding before the wind, heralding yet another raid for cattle and other prize items. Indeed, MacNeil even took to raiding the ships of Good Queen Bess of England. These attacks came to a head when she applied to King James to use whatever influence he had to bring MacNeil to justice. In answer, King James sent Ruaraidh MacKenzie of Kintail to bring the pirate to Edinburgh.

MacNeil was captured by a subterfuge and despatched to Edinburgh under guard. At the trial, before the King, he was asked to explain his piratical deeds. MacNeil replied that he had only attacked the English ships in revenge for what Queen Elizabeth had done to the King's mother (Mary Queen of Scots was beheaded under the authority of Elizabeth). King James was so dumbfounded that he could hardly continue the trial. MacNeil was left to return to Barra on condition that he recognised MacKenzie of Kintail as his overlord and paid him an annual tribute of £40. The MacNeils held Barra until 1827 when its ownership passed to the Gordons of Cluny Castle in Aberdeenshire, an event which heralded much social upheaval and hard times suffered by the Barra folk.

In the next few centuries many of the chiefs of the clans were confirmed in their land holdings by royal charter. Before this happened lands changed hands at a bewildering rate, as clans fought neighbours for possessions. So far as the Western Isles were concerned, Lewis came into the ownership of the MacKenzies of Seaforth, a mainland clan, replacing the long rule of the MacLeods. MacDonald of Sleat, in Skye, became the owner of North Uist. Barra was retained by the MacNeils. Harris fell into the hands of the MacLeods of Dunvegan, on Skye. And Clanranald owned much of South Uist. Thus the greater part of the Long Island was owned by a handful of men whose power over the islesfolk was virtually absolute. They, in turn, rented out their possessions to tenants in return for cash and the provision of personal and military services. As many of these tenants were the immediate relatives of the chief, they ensured that the land was always under the jurisdiction of the clan's main family.

As for the common folk, they were simply tenants at will, paying rents mostly in crops and services, for this was a cashless society. They had no security of tenure, a situation which was to place them at the mercy of later landlords who decided to clear the people off the land in favour of sheep and deer farms and sporting estates.

As for the chiefs themselves, they lived in a fairly grand style in castles which were rather less than the magnificent fortified structures which were common on the Scottish mainland. Their castles tended to be ancient and hardly provided for bodily comforts. They were often built of rubble heavily bedded in mortar, with double-skinned walls a few feet thick. The main castles in the Western Isles were at Stornoway (MacLeods of Lewis), Borve, Benbecula (Clanranald), Ormacleit, South Uist (Clanranald) and Kismul, Barra (the MacNeils).

Stornoway Castle, now a pile of rubble under Stornoway's harbour facilities, was, according to tradition, built by the Nicolsons of Lewis who were of Norse extraction and who held sway in the islands before the MacLeods. Records are scanty, with the first documentary mention of the structure being in 1506, when it was besieged and captured by the Earl of Huntly. At that time the castle may have been 200 years old. Its walls were thick enough to withstand the bombardment and other attacks. In 1554 it was again under attack, this time by the Earl of Argyll, and 50 years later was once more battered by artillery, by which time the building had succumbed to its harsh treatment. The main reason for the attacks was the MacLeods, who tended to pay little respect to the authority of the King in Edinburgh. In a manuscript dated 1595 mention is made of 'Lewis pertains to MacLeod of the Lewis, who being an old man famous for the massacring of his own kinsmen', which indicates that a certain state of lawlessness existed and that the MacLeods were at loggerheads with each other.

By the time the Commonwealth ruled over Britain, and Stornoway was occupied by English forces, the castle was not worth taking over, for the English Colonel Cobbet, who took command of Lewis, built a separate garrison for his soldiers. The castle ruins remained visible until 1882 when they were removed to make way for a new pier installation. A plaque on the Maritime Buildings in Stornoway commemmorates the site of the

Ormacleit Castle, South Uist

ancient castle. A few very old photographs still exist which show part of a
tumbledown tower sitting on top of a pile of rubble.

The ruins of Borve Castle in Benbecula reflect its age. Built around
1350 by Amy MacRuari, first wife of John, Lord of the Isles, it was an
impressive structure three storeys high, of which the uppermost was the
great hall. This same Amy spent much of her time commissioning the
building of various chapels throughout the islands. As with Stornoway
Castle, there are few references available which allow the whole history of
Borve to be told. It was, however, the principal island stronghold of
Clanranald and, as the chief's residence, it was a focal point of power,
learning and culture in the extended network of the Gaelic social order –
within which Clanranald played a leading role. The castle was abandoned
at the beginning of the eighteenth century, in favour of the new castle built
at Ormacleit in South Uist.

Ormacleit Castle was built as an unfortified house in the early eighteenth century by Allan MacDonald, who fell mortally wounded at the Battle of Sheriffmuir in 1715. In his youth he had been a fugitive from Cromwell and took refuge in France. After the Restoration he returned to South Uist and decided to replace Borve Castle as a residence. He employed a French architect and masons to build Ormacleit, who took the best part of seven years to complete the work. It only lasted another seven years as it was burnt to the ground on the very eve that Allan MacDonald was killed at Sheriffmuir.

Of Kismul Castle, standing on a small rocky islet at Castlebay, there is much more to tell. Its main tower dates from about 1120. The earliest structure is thought to have been a great curtain wall, adjusted to the contours of the rock base. Midway, on the eastern front, was the only entrance defended by a portcullis. Later, a square keep tower was erected on the south-eastern side, the original entrance being blocked up and a new portal being made close to the keep so that it could be kept under surveillance at all times. Within the courtyard are a hall, chapel and other buildings now restored. Both the curtain wall and the tower retain the early medieval arrangements for crowning the wall-heads, with wooden galleries designed for defence. A conspicuous feature of the masonry is the bands of large stones up-ended or set on edge, with broad flat surfaces to the exterior. This technique was common in the Hebrides to reduce the penetration of rain and seawater.

Home for the MacNeils, Kismul Castle was reduced to a ruin in 1795, when a fire swept through the building and destroyed the floors, roofs and wooden galleries. The family then went on to the island of Barra to live in their new 'seat' at Eoligarry, to play the role of landed gentry rather than warrior chiefs. Then, in 1838, with their finances in disarray, they sold out and moved away from Barra. With the death of General Roderick MacNeil, the succession passed to a branch of the family living in Canada. The 45th clan chief, an American architect, began a restoration of Kismul in 1938 which was completed in 1970 and is now, once again, clan home of the MacNeils.

If one sets aside the petty internal squabbles between clans in the Western Isles and, in particular, on Lewis – where local traditions tell of skirmishes between the Morrisons and the MacAulays, and between the MacLeods fighting among themselves – the islands were generally free from outside interference. Being remote with the only access to them by sea routes, they escaped much of the bloody upheavals which occurred in the sixteenth and seventeenth centuries on mainland Scotland. But, though isolated, they were not forgotten. The island of Lewis had its name bandied about in the same breath as 'profit'; that, coupled with the fact that MacLeod of Lewis was making a nuisance of himself – with the island

An outcrop of Lewisian gneiss retains its sharp outlines despite the pummelling waves (over)

Iain MacNeil, Chief and Landlord of most of Barra. Kismul Castle can be seen in the background

in a state of anarchy – it was inevitable that the royal court in Edinburgh would apply its authority to settling the problem.

For some time King James VI (James I of England) had been concerned that much of the rents due to him by MacLeod were long ovedue. In addition, reports that Lewismen had 'given themselves over to all kynd of barbaritie and inhumanitie . . . voyd of ony knawledge of God or His religion' meant that his royal authority had to be asserted. Another factor came into his considerations. Reports suggested that Lewis was something of an El Dorado, not so much in gold but in natural produce. Lewis was described as being 'inrychit with ane incredibill fertilitie of cornis and store of fischeingis and utheris necessaris, surpassing far the plenty of any pairt of the inland'. The truth was much less than that, though the sea was rich indeed. The solution to the problem of Lewis was to launch a programme of civilisation, which was broad enough in its interpretation of the word to cover up other motives. Thus emerged a scheme which, in name, has gone down in history as the 'Fife Adventurers'.

A contract was drawn up between the King and a body of gentlemen, largely from Fife, who, inspired by the exaggerated reports, were keen to have a share of the rich pickings thought to be gathered in Lewis. The Adventurers landed on Lewis in November 1598 to fulfil their end of the bargain, which included the 'ruiting out the barbarous inhabitantis'. In effect, the expedition was to be punitive in character.

Cold though the weather was at that time of the year, the Fifers had a hot welcome, with the MacLeods giving them a stiff warm-up fight. However, the few hundred well-armed and disciplined soldiers brought by the expedition soon wore down the native opposition and the 'Adventurers' managed to gain a foothold in Stornoway. Their first task was to build a fortification to protect themselves from attack. They then constructed houses of stone, timber and turf to create what one report described as a 'prettie toun'. But food ran short. Believing the reports that there was much milk and honey on Lewis, they had brought with them minimal stores, which were soon exhausted. The cold weather added to their troubles, which included an epidemic of dysentery. Matters went so badly for them that they were forced to send a messenger south to ask for help. But the messenger was captured by the MacLeods at sea. Another message was sent, this time carried by a party of armed soldiers, whom the Adventurers could ill afford to lose.

No sooner had they disappeared over the horizon when the barricades were attacked by Chief Neil MacLeod with 'two hundred barbarius, bludie, and wiket Hielandmen' who managed to despatch 22 members of the camp, burn property and made off with horses, cattle and sheep. A desperate situation arose, which required desperate and unorthodox tactics. The Adventurers appealed to Neil MacLeod and managed to persuade him to come over to their side. Needless to say, the move hardly pleased the other members of Neil's family. Indeed, so much did Neil swing the other way that he was instrumental in treacherously capturing his brother Murdoch, who had made himself particularly obnoxious to the Adventurers. Twelve of his followers were immediately beheaded and their heads sent in a sack to Edinburgh, to reinforce a report on progress. Murdoch himself was sent to Fife (where else?) as a prisoner and, after a trial, was hanged at St Andrews.

Neil MacLeod, however, proved to be a fractious and slippery friend. He often quarrelled with the Adventurers and eventually became their deadly enemy once more to wreak some harsh proof of his turncoat ways. In a cloud of despair the Adventurers left Lewis, to return in 1605, only to meet the same determined opposition to their plans. A third attempt made in 1610 to resolve the situation again failed and the Fife Adventurers finally sold their charter rights to a man who had looked on the Lewis drama as an interesting prelude to his own main chance. He was Kenneth

MacKenzie of Kintail who, though supposedly a friend of the Crown and the colonists, was actually scheming behind their backs. Now, in effective possession of Lewis, it took him only two years to reduce the MacLeods into accepting him as the new owner of the island. Once the royal charter was signed, the MacKenzies became the new overlords of Lewis, to remain in control until the early years of the nineteenth century. While all this was going on in the rarefied atmosphere of the aristocracy, what of the common folk? Apart from those men who were part of the chiefs' armed tails, there were many whose daily life was solely concerned with the toil needed to produce food and animals and to catch fish for a welcome change of diet. But they were also under specific obligations to whoever owned or rented the land on which they lived and worked, which included payments in kind or in a certain number of days service each year. A few of the more privileged were small tenants in their own right, holding land for specific terms varying from, say, five years to 'a lifetime and eleven years'. The common folk, then, were effectively peasants, who sometimes banded their interests together to obtain a townland, thereby increasing productivity. A township consisted of a number of poor dwellings which were close to inbye, or arable land. This land was abandoned during the summer months, to allow it to freshen up for the wintering of beasts, and use was made of moorland and summer pastures. On these pastures rough houses were built, known as shielings, the ruins of which can still be seen scattered all over the islands. Peat cutting was also done during this time to provide fuel for the winter.

The crops from the land included oats and barley (this was before the days of the ubiquitous potato); livestock included horses, cattle, sheep, pigs and goats. It was cattle, however, which received the greatest attention, for they constituted an important form of economic wealth. Cattle provided dairy products, meat and hides and, beyond that, could be used to pay off debts or sold for cash. In fact, the Western Isles in the seventeenth and eighteenth centuries could produce little else that could generate hard cash. By the seventeenth century the cattle trade from the islands was extensive, each year seeing great black streams of cattle being moved from the islands into Skye and on to the Scottish mainland, all under the control of professional drovers. The main trading centres, or trysts, were at Crieff and Falkirk in central Scotland.

While the common folk had little need for money, it was a different tale with the landowners. Their taste for fine living had increased over the decades, and this taste had to be catered for with items which required the payment of hard cash. In particular, their fondness for imported wines and spirits, which often came in ship-loads, required considerable sums of money for their purchase. Fine clothes and lavish furnishings sucked whatever cash was generated in the islands outwards and left little or none for investment in more local projects. Even allowing for the fact that little cash was paid by tenantry, the incomes in 1644 of Clanranald and similar

The local history museum at Craigston in Barra

chiefs were considerable: some £9000 per annum. That of MacLeod of
Dunvegan on Skye was assessed at around £15,000. It was this constant
need for money, mainly to be spent in the flesh-pots of the sophisticated
south, which eventually burst the bonds between chief and clansmen,
which thrust apart age-long bonds of loyalty. In due time estates had to be
sold to assuage creditors. New landowners entered the scene with scant
regard for the common folk and proceded to clear them off the land, to
write a terrible chapter in the history of the Highlands and Islands.

While clearances took place in Lewis and in Harris, they were nothing
to the situation with existed in the southern isles, and in South Uist and
Barra in particular.

The end of the Clanranald family in the Uists began in 1794, when the
chief succeeded as a minor to estates which paid him an annual £25,000 in
rents and which had been in the family for five centuries. But, by 1827,
after some three decades devoted to high living in London, and

representing an English rotten borough in Parliament, he found himself on the verge of bankruptcy. His agents tried their best to wring every last penny out of the estates with little success. In 1837, South Uist was sold for £84,000 to Lt-Col John Gordon of Cluny in Aberdeenshire. Barra was sold in 1838 to the same Gordon, and Benbecula followed in 1839.

The immediate concern of the Gordon family was to realise their new-won assets, but this could not be done while these estates were crowded with an indigenous population. To create profits it was necessary to form large farms which, in turn, required the removal of those who lived on the land. As the latter were tenants at will, the way was clear for the owners to remove them. Thus started a long period of harassment accompanied by much cruelty and inhumanity.

Matters came to a head in the 1840s, when the potato crop failed and the islesfolk found starvation staring them in their faces. A Government investigator, touring round the west coast of Scotland to assess the situation, found many scenes of indescribable horror. He reported on the estates of Gordon '. . . an awful reflection . . . that at this moment the wealthy inheritor of this island is not employing the poor population' and predicted that '. . . scenes will occur in South Uist, Barra and Benbecula which would be disgraceful to his name, and injurious to the reputation of Great Britain'. Gordon was then written to by a Government official who threatened '. . . to interpose in favour of the sufferers . . . leaving Parliament to decide whether or not you should be legally responsible for the pecuniary consequences of this just and necessary intervention'. Gordon reacted by starting work on the estates which was paid for by doling out quantities of meal to alleviate the situation in which his tenants found themselves.

But the year 1847 again saw the devastation of crops by bad weather and the dreaded potato blight ruining the scanty sowings of potatoes. Reports came in to Government sources of the pathetic conditions in South Uist: '. . . The scene of wretchedness which we witnessed as we entered on the estate of Col Gordon was deplorable, nay, heart-rending. On the beach the whole population of the country seemed to be met, gathering the precious cockles . . . I never witnessed such countenances – starvation on many faces – the children with their melancholy looks, big looking knees, shrivelled legs, hollow eyes, swollen-like bellies – God help them, I never did witness such wretchedness.'

Between 1849 and 1851 upwards of 2000 persons were forcibly shipped from South Uist and Barra to Quebec: the owners' answer to the problem. Others were induced to embark voluntarily, under promise that they were to be conveyed free of all expense to Upper Canada where, on arrival, Government agents would give them work and grant them land. These conditions were not fulfilled. They were turned adrift at Quebec and thence compelled to beg their way to Upper Canada. The Canadian newspapers teemed with accounts of the miseries endured by those unfortunate emigrants, whose misfortunes were aggravated by the fact that they could speak only Gaelic. The 'Quebec Times' had this to say in 1851:

> We noticed in our last the deplorable condition of the 600 paupers who were sent to this country from the Kilrush Unions. We have today a still more dismal picture to draw. Many of our readers may not be aware that there lives such a personage as Colonel Gordon, proprietor of large estates, South Uist and Barra, in the Highlands of Scotland. We are sorry to be obliged to introduce him to their notice under circumstances which will not give them a very favourable opinion of his character and heart. It appears that tenants of the above-mentioned estates were on the verge of starvation, and had probably become an eyesore to the gallant colonel. He decided on shipping them to America.

Those who were unwilling to accept the Colonel's promises found themselves hunted as fugitives. Not a few men were attacked and rendered senseless before they were thrown, with arms bound, on to the waiting ships. Members of families were torn apart and put on to different ships with different destinations in the Americas. Others managed to escape to the hills but eventually succumbed to the Colonel's agents through hunger.

In February 1851 a group of 61 destitutes made their slow way from Barra to Inverness and sat down in front of the Town House to see what the authorities would do for them. About 40 of them were sent to the parish poorhouse, while the remainder were accommodated in lodgings. After a few days the group drifted eastwards, hoping to find employment in the fisheries on the Buchan coast. Later, faced with fresh arrivals, the Inverness Inspector of the Poor tried to recover the cost of their upkeep from the Barra Parochial Board. But the latter pointed out that they were not responsible for the able-bodied, and further demanded that any of their charges under the care of the Inspector be sent back to Barra immediately. Eventually these wanderers from Barra, rather than return to their native island, found work near Inverness, where they lived in great poverty.

It was inevitable that such scenes as these were to turn the tide against Highland and Island landowners. Though some lairds spent money in order to alleviate the circumstances of their tenants, they were few and far between.

By the 1870s, throughout the Highlands and Islands, a movement was generated which advocated land reform by whatever means might be thought suitable and available. The movement became politicized, which added no little strength to the demands of the class of people who were soon to be enshrined in the Statute Books of Great Britain as 'crofters'. 'There is nothing in history so absolutely mean as the eviction of the Highlanders by chiefs solely indebted for every inch of land they ever held to the strong arms and trusty blades of the progenitors of those whom the effeminate and ungrateful chiefs of the nineteenth century have so ruthlessly oppressed, evicted and despoiled.' So said Alexander MacKenzie, a prominent figure in the agitation of the 1870s to win security of tenure and legal recognition for the crofter population. Statements like that were bound to set the heather on fire; and so they did.

The seeds of revolt against their intolerable conditions were initially sown in 1874, by crofters on the remote island of Bernera in Lewis. At that time the whole of Lewis was the possession of Sir James Matheson, who had made his fortune in the Far East – with no small portion of it earned through trafficking in opium. Matheson did, in fact, spend much money on various enterprises on the island, including opening up roads. But he had little interest in the residual population. Contact with tenants was left to his factor, Donald Munro. One crofter giving evidence before the Napier Commission, appointed by Royal Warrant to look into crofting conditions, stated that he was convinced that Munro's policy 'from the first day of his factorship to the last was to extirpate the people of Lewis so far as he could'. If that was not quite Munro's intention, the statement at least indicated that he had a fearful standing in the minds of the Lewis folk.

Munro's Nemesis arrived on the Lewis scene in 1872, when crofters on Bernera island were told that their traditional summer grazings were to be taken over to form part of a new estate and that other land would be offered in compensation. This land, however, was not as good, but the crofters agreed to the arrangement and, in addition, agreed to build a new stone dyke to separate the new grazings from the old. Two years' hard work went into that dyke, seven miles long, which was rewarded in 1874 by Munro appearing on the scene to say that a new decision had been made: their newly acquired grazings were to be changed again. The crofters vented their feelings in no uncertain manner and a situation arose which Munro countered by sending the Volunteers from Stornoway, of which he was the Commanding Officer (among a countless number of other hats he wore as factor to Lewis). There was the threat of evictions, even though none of the crofters was in arrears of rent.

The day of reckoning arrived, with estate officials armed with 58 summonses of removal. They moved throughout the whole community with no hindrance until the evening, when they were met by a crowd of boys and girls who threw grass divots at them. This reception was met with a comment from the Sheriff Officer: 'If I had a gun with me there would be some of the women in Bernera tonight lamenting their sons.'

The following morning the crofters met the estate officials and demanded to know the name of the officer who had threatened their children. A scuffle ensued, in which the Sheriff Officer had his coat torn. He trundled back to Stornoway and made a complaint of assault which led to the arrest of three Bernera crofters.

Other crofters immediately went to see Sir James Matheson in Lews Castle at Stornoway. He expressed surprise at the intention of Munro to evict 58 crofters. Munro countered by saying he did not think his intention was a matter of sufficient importance to lay before his employer. At the trial the three arrested crofters were acquitted and Munro's methods came in for severe criticism. The Sheriff Officer was fined 21 shillings for assault.

That little affair was the beginning of the end of a long period during which lairds and factors ruled like tyrants over the Highland people. The trial highlighted the invidious position of crofters and paved the way for a decade or so of activity and agitation which culminated in the appointment of a Royal Commission, the Napier Commission, to look into the conditions of crofters in the Highlands and Islands.

The Commission took both oral and written evidence from both sides and ended up with a Report running to over 3000 pages of answers given orally to some 46,000 questions, in addition to written evidence. Here, in fact, was a history of trial and tribulation created by the people out of their own mouths and describing their parlous situation.

The Crofters Act was passed by Parliament in 1886, to give crofters security of tenure among other advantages and which also curtailed the methods used by factors to evict people from their homes and land. But the land question was far from being over.

There was still a great deal of pressure on landlords to make land available for a large number of people who found themselves without in the provisions of the 1886 Act – the cottars. Homeless, they had no recognizable piece of land which they could cultivate and provide themselves with subsistence living. This was the situation on Barra, which example will serve to illustrate what happened elsewhere in the Western Isles, in Benbecula and in Lewis.

At the turn of the century Barra was overcrowded with land-hungry crofters agitating for room to move, to live and make their living. In 1901 the Government, under what it chose to call 'excessive pressure', bought 3000 acres to give 58 crofters new holdings, which still left half the landless cottars, or squatters, unprovided for. These folk applied for holdings on the nearby island of Vatersay which was a large farm, occupied by one farmer and his family. Again, the Government were forced into buying 60 acres on Vatersay to be divided among 51 crofters. But the ground was poor and even potatoes failed to produce a significant yield. Matters came to a head with the crofters threatening to take more land, by force if need be. But another tactic was used. One cottar from Barra went over to Vatersay and, with the help of friends, erected a wooden dwelling; the house was up and thatched in a few hours and a fire lit. It is an old law in Scotland which states that if a house can be erected, roofed and fired between sunrise and sunset on the same day, the houseowner can take possession of the land. Other cottars followed this example and took over land, with cattle and sheep to stock it.

These Vatersay 'raiders' were brought to trial and given six months' imprisonment. But the affair raised such a public outcry that they were given an early release.

The owner of Vatersay, Lady Gordon Cathcart, refused to co-operate in the formation of new holdings on the island, and the affair ended in 1909 with the Board of Agriculture buying Vatersay to turn the whole of the island over to crofting holdings.

Many similar takeovers of land were common throughout the Western Isles. The land at Nunton on Benbecula was assumed by crofters in 1923 in a land raid. The estate factor, in the employ of Lady Gordon Cathcart, wrote: 'the crofterization of Nunton will make it practically impossible for Lady Cathcart to sell Benbecula should she wish to do so as the whole island would then be under crofters'. In essence, that meant that if people were on land, they would detract from its value and so make it worth less on an open market than if the land were depopulated.

The years following World War I also saw mass emigration to Canada and the United States. Hundreds of young men and women, seeing no future for themselves in the Western Isles, left Barra, the Uists and Lewis, boarded huge ocean-going liners in droves. The effect of this draining of vital young blood, enterprise and initiative left its mark for many decades. Unable to pursue their traditional crofting way of life, they found new work in such places as the car factories of Detroit.

The islanders still living often reflect on these years of the Twenties with two themes running through their reminiscences: widespread hardship and mass emigration. Particularly in the southern isles, the controversy which surrounded the emigration schemes advertised by the Canadian Pacific Railway – under whose promotions several hundreds of emigrants from Barra, Benbecula and South Uist sailed for the New World – still evokes bitter comments.

4. Island portraits

Lewis

Though twinned to each other by a narrow isthmus, Lewis and Harris are regarded as being separate islands. Lewis is the largest and most northerly in the island chain and, in some respects, it is often difficult to appreciate that one is indeed on an island. With over 70 per cent of the Western Isles population living in Lewis, and with the headquarters of the Local Authority also based in Stornoway, there is a gravitational pull towards the north part of the island chain which, despite efforts made by the Authority to counter the trend by measures of de-centralization, still tends to create problems. Linear structures, whatever their nature, have always produced polarization.

Distances often surprise visitors. From the Butt of Lewis to the Harris border by road is some 80 miles. By road from Tiumpan Head on the Eye Peninsula to Breanish in Uig to the west is over 50 miles. Virtually all crofting townships in Lewis are scattered round the coast, or at least within sight or smell of the sea. Achmore, the excepton, is an inland settlement. The main topographical features of Lewis are its moors, low rolling hills, infinite variety of coastal scenery and high hills – almost small mountains – in the south-western part of the island. The eastern coast is generally rocky with deep and serrated shorelines of sea lochs, dotted with islands. The western coastline is steeper to the sea in many places, with sheer cliffs occurring at Gallan Head which occasionally give way to sudden falls to sea level. Uig Bay, where the Red River runs into the sea, is a wide sweep of white sand.

Added interest on the eastern side is offered by the Eye Peninsula, which is tied to the main island mass of Lewis by a narrow strip of sand dunes which have had to be protected against erosion by sea walls. On the north side of the isthmus is Broad Bay, a wide sweep of shallow water which, despite illegal trawling, still retains a reputation as a fish breeding ground. Machair land on the Lewis coasts is not as plentiful as in the Southern Isles, but does occur mainly on the western side and to the north of Stornoway. Freshwater lochs abound in Lewis with reasonably sized brown trout. Though, in theory, fishing for brown trout is free, some estates require licences to be purchased. Local advice is always valuable to discover the situation in a particular area.

The Butt of Lewis lighthouse in the 1940s

Lewis is divided into a number of Parishes. Some are densely populated, such as those of Ness and Point (on the Eye Peninsula). Others are less so, with townships scattered almost at random. All are connected by a fairly good road system, though some minor roads are still single-track – which requires judicious use of passing places to allow other traffic to advance or overtake.

The most northerly parish is Ness which, as its name implies, reflects its Norse origins. Indeed, the men of Ness tend to be as skilled seamen as were their distant forebears, and even today demonstrate their mastery of the sea in an annual exercise called the 'Guga Hunt'.

Some forty miles north of Lewis lie two remote islands, North Rona and Sulasgeir. Rona is the larger of the two and boasts a green salt-seasoned sward. It was once populated mainly by residents who looked after sheep placed on the island for fattening. Sir James Matheson, who bought Lewis in 1844, once offered the island to the Government for use as a penal settlement, a kind of British Devil's Island. The offer was refused. But it is Sulasgeir, some 12 miles west of North Rona, which has a special place in the seafaring history of the men of Ness. Though often called an island it is, in fact, little more than a large sea rock, half a mile long and 200 yards at its maximum breadth. There is scarcely any soil on Sulasgeir. That lack is made up by the rock's role as one of the most important breeding grounds for gannets, with some 5000 breeding pairs on Sulasgeir, which they share with other bird species such as kittiwakes, guillemots, puffins, Leach's petrel and fulmars. The rock's name sula (solan goose) and sgeir (rock) gives the clue to its importance for Ness.

One of the earliest accounts written about the Western Isles was by Dean Monro, who visited the islands in 1549. His description of Sulasgeir mentions that the men of Ness sailed in their small craft to 'fetche hame thair boatful of dry wild fowls with wild fowl fedderis'. How long before 1549 the Nessmen had sailed to Sulasgeir each year to collect the young gannets for food and feathers is not known, but it may be assumed that it had been a tradition for centuries. That tradition is still carried on today. A report written in 1797 says: 'There is in Ness a most venturous set of people who for a few years back, at the hazard of their lives, went there in an open six-oared boat without even the aid of a compass'. Excellent seamanship was certainly essential for the success of these expeditions – rowing across 40 miles of turbulent Atlantic water was no pleasure cruise.

The flesh of the young gannet or 'guga' is regarded as a delicacy in Ness today though, for others, it is an acquired taste. Even so, it was a popular meat in earlier times in Scotland. In the sixteenth century it was served at the table of Scots kings and was a favourite with the wealthy as a 'whet' or appetizer before main meals. In the autumn of each year, a hardy team of Nessmen set sail for Sulasgeir to kill around 2000 young birds and bring home their catch about a week later, to meet an eager crowd of customers, who snap up as many of the birds as they can. The demand is often so great that the birds have to be rationed out to ensure that each person does not go without a taste of guga.

This annual cull of birds has been the focus of attention of bird protectionists, who recently have tried to ban the cull completely. But tradition dies hard and the Sulasgeir trip still goes on, with a special dispensation written into the 1954 Wild Birds Protection Act by a Statutory Order, which allows the Nessmen to continue their taste both for adventure and for the guga.

Crofting is the main activity here in this area, given a welcome boost with the machair land, which helps productivity. In Port of Ness there is an unusual enterprise of many decades' standing: boat-building. Not only is it unusual, but there are echoes of the Norse origins of the folk hereabouts. The boat type built here is called a sgoth, with its design modelled on the style of the Shetland sixern (Old Norse: sexaeringr), a clinker built vessel of fir and fastened with iron. The method of construction was similar to that of the older Viking ships. Originally the vessel was undecked, but a half deck was provided at a later date. One of the last boats of this type in existence is the 'Jubilee', which was rescued from an overgrown sea of grass in the grounds of a Stornoway house.

Alginate factory, a Co-op in Keose, Lewis

Rescued from this ill-deserved fate, the 'Jubilee' has been completely restored by a band of enthusiasts, led by members of the family which has built boats for decades, the MacLeods. The craft sails the Ness waters each summer and, when seen in full sail, must revive many memories of the old days when the sail was king of the seas.

Of particular interest is the church of St Moluag, not far from the Butt of Lewis lighthouse. The first church built on the site dated from the sixth century when St Moluag, a companion of St Columba, founded a chapel here. The present building dates from the twelfth century and was erected by Olaf the Black during the Norse occupation. The church was far famed for its influence in the healing of lunatics, the cure being, among other strange treatments, to drink water from the nearby well and then walk seven times round the church. The patient was then bound hand and foot and left in front of the altar all night. The church remained in good repair until about 1630 when it was abandoned and left to deteriorate. However, it was restored and re-dedicated to St Moluag in 1912 and is now the property of the Scottish Episcopal Church. The stone cross is of seventh century workmanship and came from the ruined chapel on the island of North Rona. A sixteenth-century alms box at the door of the church came from Flanders, by what route is not exactly known.

The west side of Lewis takes in a number of densely populated crofting townships: Barvas, Shawbost, Bragar and Carloway. At Carloway, in one of its small village settlements, is Garenin, a short street of old black houses, much in need of proper restoration to present an idea of what life was like in Lewis many years ago. At Arnol, some miles north of Shawbost, stands a restored black house which was occupied up until about 20 years ago. The house features throw much light on the history and social background of such buildings in the Western Isles.

It contains under one thatched roof the domestic accommodation, a byre and a barn, with a small stockyard outside, and is typical of the dwellings once common in Lewis until a few decades ago. At Shawbost an old church has been converted into a museum, which contains many interesting relics of bygone days in Lewis. Started as a school project, the collection has grown rather like Topsy, but still retains the essence of the children's conception of life in the past.

On the east coast of Lewis lie a number of crofting townships with the sea in close proximity, from Tolsta, through Coll, Gress, Back and Tong, all names which give away their Norse origins, though Tong as a community is a village of more recent standing, its folk having been cleared from other parts of Lewis and Harris during the last century or so. Also on the east coast is the Point district, one of the most densely populated in Lewis. Situated on the Eye Peninsula, there are a number of visible witnesses to a long inhabitation from prehistoric and Norse times.

South of Stornoway is the parish of Lochs, so called because of the large number of freshwater lochs and a number of arms of the sea which stretch inland. North of the parish are a few close-knit crofting townships; to the south the villages are more scattered, with a few suffering from depopulation and an ageing population.

It takes a car journey of some forty miles from Stornoway to get into the parish of Uig on the south-west of Lewis. Here we enter mountainous country, though the coast offers many good stretches of sand, particularly at Ardroil.

It was near here, in 1831, that a small structure was uncovered in a sandbank by an exceptionally high tide, to reveal the now famous 'Lewis Chessmen'. These were 78 pieces belonging to at least eight incomplete chess sets. Dating from the twelfth century, they are of Norse origin and made from walrus ivory. The figures are mainly church dignitaries, with one figure portraying the fanatical warrior of the Norse, the beserk or lead-biter, still commemorated in the surname common in the northern isles: Ledbitter. The original pieces are now to be seen in the National

Loch Fada, Griminish, Benbecula (over)

Land reclamation at Garry beach, North Tolsta, Lewis

Museum of Antiquities in Edinburgh and in the Ivory Room of the British Museum.

Stornoway

Of all the ports on the deeply serrated west coast of Scotland, Stornoway possesses one of the finest locations. Set in the crook of an inner harbour, and protected from the turbulent waters of the Minch by two effective land arms, the town is a natural haven. So it must have been when the Vikings first arrived to name the place Steering-bay. From their times to the present, Stornoway has grown slowly but surely into a large, attractive town, enhanced in its aspect not only by its island rhythms, lent to it by its moorland hinterland, but also by the magnificent woodlands which surround Lews Castle. When the Fife Adventurers arrived to colonize Lewis and raise the islanders from their supposedly barbarous state under the MacLeods of Lewis, the town was but a poor settlement of rude dwellings. As the benefits of civilization were perceived the settlement grew, albeit fitfully, into a burgh with accruing status, so much so that it entered the pages of Scotland's history and eventually that of the world.

In the reign of Queen Elizabeth, when England and Sweden plotted against the Scottish Crown, it was in Stornoway that the emissaries of both countries met to discuss tactics. Later, in 1719, a council of war was held in Stornoway to plan the overthrow of the Hanoverian dynasty of Britain. The town was of importance to the army of Cromwell's Commonwealth, who secured their defences by building a barracks and storehouses. A ground plan of the fortifications survives in Worcester College, Oxford University, with an estimated date of 1653.

In 1746, after his defeat at the Battle of Culloden, Prince Charles Edward, a fugitive from English redcoats in the Western Isles, stayed for some days at the farm of Kildun, on Arnish just across the Bay. As he watched the twinkling lights of the town, while his friends tried to charter a ship to take him to France, he must have pondered on his fate and his future and reflected on the day, a year before, when he set foot on the Prince's Strand on the island of Eriskay. Though he was unsuccessful in his attempts to hire a ship at Stornoway, he retraced his steps southwards to find his salvation in Flora MacDonald of South Uist.

With little but bleak moorland behind it, Stornoway has had to look to the sea for its prosperity. Not for nothing did the coat of arms of the now defunct Stornoway Burgh have three fish emblazoned on the shield over the motto 'God's Providence is our Inheritance'. And, certainly, the providence was twofold: both in the rich waters of the Minch and in the role of the town as a major trading port. But the sea has also been a hard mistress to satisfy. On New Year's Eve 1918 the *Iolaire* struck the dreaded Beasts of Holm, sharp-edged rocks just outside the entrance to Stornoway Harbour. Crammed with Lewismen returning from the war, soldiers and seamen, the vessel quickly took in water and sank beneath the waves. Bad weather hampered the efforts of many to swim to the shore, though one man, needless to say a MacLeod from the sea-faring Ness community, managed to get ashore with a line, a lifeline as Fate would have it for those who took advantage of this route to safety. But for 200 others it was a watery reward for the horrors they experienced on the muddy battlefields of France and Belgium. Hardly a household in Lewis and Harris escaped the touch of tragedy, still remembered today on the gravestones in the island's cemeteries.

Because of the opposition of established Burghs on the Scottish mainland, who feared trade might be diverted from their own commercial operations, Stornoway never quite achieved the status of a Royal Burgh, having to content itself with being a Burgh of Barony. Even so, the town's leading lights determined that relative isolation should be no barrier to progress. By the eighteenth century a lively trade existed between Stornoway and the Baltic ports, Scandinavia, Holland and France, with ships importing wine, fine goods and luxuries and exporting meat, fish, hides and other island produce. During the first half of the nineteenth

Carloway, Lewis

century fish were being exported as far away as the Mediterranean ports. Foreign sailing ships were thus a common sight in Stornoway Bay, and these required careening and repair. It was thus a natural development when an enterprising local started up a ship-building yard, which turned out many fine vessels for owners as far away as Liverpool. The scent of tar and pitch, the crunching of a busy grindstone, the shaping of a ship's timbers, the steaming of her planks, the driving of pins and bolts, the music of the mallet and caulking-iron, the buzz from the saw-pits – they all gave the town a sense of close relationship with the sea.

Not only that, but many island and townsfolk looked to the sea for careers, from deck-hands to captains. Indeed, many families depended wholly on the sea for their livelihood and became legends in their own lifetimes. Family names like MacDonald, Ryrie, Morison, MacKenzie and MacIver were to be found as captains and skippers of some of the best sailing ships on the world's oceans: like the *Sir Launcelot*, *Assaye*, and other fast clippers which brought tea from China and wool from Australia and New Zealand.

One of the ships built at the Stornoway Slip, the town's boatyard, was the famous clipper *Lady Hood MacKenzie*. In her time she became well known on the China route as one of the fastest tea clippers. She was almost entirely manned by a Lewis crew and officers. At one time last century it was well nigh impossible to walk the streets of Stornoway without brushing against a sea captain home from a long trip of sometimes a year's duration. This tradition of obtaining the highest command at sea has been carried on even in this century; an example is the appointment in the 1960s of Captain Donald Maclean of Ness, Lewis, as Commodore Captain of the Cunard Line. This was an appropriate appointment for it was a Lewis family, the MacIvers of Uig and Liverpool, which had a great deal to do with the formation of the Line. The MacIver family, in their early days, ran a petty smack between Loch Roag, on the west of Lewis,

Carloway: a view of the quay and crofters' fields

A view of Stornoway, with Lews Castle dominating the scene

and Campbeltown. Later, brothers David and Charles MacIver operated packet ships on the Clyde coast, with the City of Glasgow Steam Packet Company, in 1844. Development was inevitable and, from the regular steamship travel across the Atlantic, formed the basis of the Cunard Line. It was stretching the long arm of coincidence rather for their partner, Sam Cunard, an American, had a surname reflecting the Gaelic words Cuan Ard (= High Seas), a more than appropriate name for a steamship company with Lewis connections.

One Lewis family whose surname became a byword in shipping circles last century was the Ryries of Stornoway, a surname which now exists only on the family tombstone in Sandwick Cemetery. The family produced, in the same generation, no fewer than three famous clipper

Offshore rig construction at Arnish, Stornoway

captains in the China trade and, indeed (how close-knit was the sea-faring community on Lewis!) captain of the first Cunarder to sail into New York. The family's first connection with the sea was Captain Alick Ryrie, who served his apprenticeship on the London convict ship *Surrey*. An inauspicious beginning, one might think; but he went on to become commander of the Cunard liner *Hibernia* when she inaugurated the first New York service in December 1847. Captain John MacKenzie Ryrie commanded the tea clippers *Cairngorm*, *Flying Spur* and the *Marian*. At one time Captain Alick was in the employ of Jardine Matheson & Co., one of the partners in the Company being Sir James Matheson, who bought Lewis in 1844. In one of his letters, he mentions seeing the Company's new clipper *Stornoway* at Wampoa, at the start of her great race with the *Chrysolite*, in which she reached the downs from Hong Kong in 107 days – her holds packed full with a fortune in tea. The master of the *Stornoway* was a Captain Robertson, another Stornoway man.

'The last of the Sea Barons' was the name given to Murdo Stewart MacDonald, a native of Bernera, Lewis. Sea Baron was the title given to the men who commanded the clippers built to bring China tea half-way across the world's seas, in fantastic times which often made the later steamships look like crippled donkeys. MacDonald's ship was the *Sir Lancelot*, considered by many to be the finest and fastest clipper ever built, even with such competition offered by two other clippers of equal fame, the *Cutty Sark* and the *Thermopylae*. His command of the *Sir Lancelot* came through one of Fate's quirks. MacDonald had been sailing

The council buildings in Stornoway

as mate on the sailing ship *Assaye*, but his time was made unbearable by the captain. On berthing in Britain, he made straight for Stornoway, determined to give up the sea. He fretted his time away until a telegram arrived from McCunn, known as The Racer of Greenock, offering him the command of a ship. MacDonald replied with a brief telegram: 'What ship?', which was answered with equal brevity: *Sir Lancelot*. Thus did he become, in his early twenties, the captain of one of the most famous ships of the sailing era.

Another Stornoway skipper who made his mark at an early age was Captain Peter Pope. During the American Civil War (1851–1855), he sailed on the Liverpool clipper barque *Emily Saint Pierre*, which was a blockade runner, carrying goods to the southern States and returning to Britain with cotton. During one voyage an American revenue cruiser hove them to, and boarded the ship under gunpoint. Most of the crew were taken off, to leave the prize crew on board with the Captain, Peter Pope, the carpenter, the bosun and the cook. During the trip to an American port, the rum keg was opened and its contents liberally fed to the prize crew, who soon got so drunk that they were overpowered and battened down in the fo'c'sle. The skeleton crew then made sail and took the ship back to Liverpool, short-handed as they were. Later, Captain

Pope was made master of the first ever four-masted full-rigged ship to be launched: the *County of Inverness*.

Perhaps typical of the varied careers of island seamen was that of Thomas MacLeod, born in Stornoway in 1872, who took part in three polar expeditions. He was with Captain Scott on the *Terra Nova* in 1910–13, then with Shackleton on the *Endurance* in 1914–17 and with Shackleton again on the *Quest* in 1921–22; on this last trip Shackleton died, while the expedition was on its way out. The explorer was buried at South Georgia, after which the team was led by Captain Frank Wilde. On the return journey, it was suggested that a cairn be erected for 'the boss', as they called Shackleton, and it fell to MacLeod to build the cairn in typical Highland fashion. When Admiral Byrd decided to mount a fourth British expedition to Antarctica, MacLeod volunteered but was too late with his application. His experience, he was told, would have been invaluable, for he had started his sea career sailing in windjammers at the age of 14. When on the expedition with Captain Scott, their ship successfully weathered a storm south of Campbell Island. The crew were on the pumps for 24 hours; with MacLeod on one shift was the man who later became Admiral Teddy Evans of Australia. On the first Shackleton expedition a ship was lost. The ice closed in quickly and pushed the ship out of the water so that she overturned, though she managed to right herself. But the pressure of ice repeated the incident and she sank. Shackleton then set out for South Georgia in an open boat to get help, leaving twenty of the crew, including MacLeod, to live for ten weeks under two upturned boats on a small spit of land until they were rescued.

When the herring fishing took off in earnest in the middle of the nineteenth century, Stornoway thrived in the exciting air of prosperity brought by the boom. The herring is a delicate fish and, once landed, had to be gutted and salted or else transformed into kippers. The trade involved literally thousands of workers and old photographs of the piers round the harbour show mountains of white-wood barrels waiting for the skilfully-gutted herring to be salted and packed for shipment direct to countries which included Germany, Scandinavia, Lithuania, Estonia and the free ports of the Baltic Sea. The following description in the local newspaper (1924) gives a glimpse of those days when herring was king:

> The myriad paraffin flares lighting up the whole quay from Bayhead to the Slip, with hundreds of deft-fingered workers bending over the herring-filled farlins, working with machine-like precision and speed at their somewhat gory task, and men and women in the yellow flare flitting about among herring barrels, all eager and intent on their work, is more than mere picturesque to the people of Stornoway. To us it is a gladsome sight, speaking of returning prosperity – after many lean years – in our staple industry. The great hauls landed since the shoals were struck have eaten up huge quantities of curing stock, so that even the best prepared firms found themselves running short of barrels and salt by last weekend. The catch of the last fortnight alone

accounted for close on 60,000 barrels, and on Saturday morning, as the boats were arriving heavily laden, it was feared that for want of stock the bulk of the catch would have to lie in the holds till Monday. Fortunately, however, this proved unnecessary, for a stock boat with a large cargo came into the harbour just as the sales were commencing for the day. It was like the arrival of a relieving column to a beleagured city.

Much of the prosperity generated by the herring fishing went into the fine buildings, still to be seen in the older parts of the town. Though few are of any intrinsic architectural interest, their features exude the confidence of their former owners in a secure future. Despite the many changes wreaked by town planners over the last couple of decades, which razed much of the older houses to the ground, there are still a few areas which reflect the atmosphere of Stornoway in former times. Along Newton Street, in particular, where many of the sea-dogs of last century lived. The houses face the waters of the harbour and one can easily imagine a captain on shore leave in an upper room, telescope to his eye, as he watched foreign sailing ships making their way to the piers, perhaps recognizing the familiar trim of a ship he may have passed in the North Atlantic.

Unlike many other Scottish burghs, Stornoway has no really old buildings. Most tend to have been built in the recent past, being less than 150 years old. The oldest extant house dates from c. 1790. The Sheriff Court House was built in the 1840s. The former Female Industrial School, built by the wife of Sir James Matheson to give young girls a chance to learn domestic crafts, was erected in 1848, and is now part of a complex of buildings which includes the house of the headmistress, now the offices and display rooms of the Lewis Museum Society. The old Town House on Stornoway's main thoroughfare, Cromwell Street, which is now a restaurant, still retains something of its nineteenth-century facade.

For all its lack of evidence of a visible ancient past, Stornoway still manages to provide the occasional echo of former times. The South Beach straddles the waterfront, where once the Fife Adventurers landed to exploit the supposed riches of Lewis. The Town Hall, a magnificent red-stone building, reflects Victorian aesthetics and is the second structure of its kind, the first having been burnt down in 1918. Part of the Town Hall is now a museum with a new art gallery, a much-needed innovation to provide the town with the opportunity to view exhibitions of painting, sculpture and photography which would not otherwise come to the island.

The industrial area of the town includes the Harris Tweed mills, which provide the initial and finishing processes for the world famous cloth, woven by crofter-weavers in their own homes. Though this industry has now shrunk, it still offers an economic sheet-anchor for the islefolk and provides a much-needed stability in the employment picture.

One last vignette which describes the Stornoway of times past. It was written by a native of the town who put into book form his reminiscences and disguised them under the title of 'Portrona', an old and affectionate

These Stornoway youths might easily blend into many towns on the mainland

name for the town: '. . . a dozen streets or more, running this way and that, as Nature and man's intelligence determined. The front of the town, looking south-westwards, follows the curve of the shore; then as an arrow from his bow shoots a street, the busy street of the town . . . Men who had led a seafaring life gave a stamp to the town. The herring fishing made our bay, our shores and our streets bright and busy for a month or two of the year . . . If you stood for half an hour in a busy Portrona shop, you could understand better what the market-place was to an ancient city. People met there not only to buy and sell, but to do a little trade in thought.'

Harris

Though joined to Lewis by a thin neck of land, Harris is vastly different in its geography. For the most part it is an infertile land, with great expanses of exposed rock outcrops. Its eastern coast is rocky and deeply indented

67

by the sea. Yet it is along this coast that most of the crofting townships are located, the result of the people's clearance from the more fertile machair land on the west coast and from many of the islands in the Sound of Harris which separates Harris from North Uist. The croft land seen here is the result of many years spent creating new soil in which to grow crops such as potatoes. What are often called 'lazybeds', raised levels of earth carefully fertilized with seaweed and often resting on bedrock, are misnamed, for these patches of ground are worked to their fullest capacity, and have been for years.

On the west coast are the magnificent stretches of machair, with vast expanses of silver sand facing the Atlantic and overlooking the now deserted island of Taransay. The north part of Harris is mountainous, with the highest peak being reached by the Clisham (2,622 ft). This is mainly deer forest, a moorland desolate and wild in character, with no trees to offer cover for the deer stock that roam in the area.

Though the MacLeods of Lewis and Harris come from the same Norse stock, the Harris branch has its historical associations more with the MacLeods of Dunvegan on Skye. As chiefs they tended to have a more humane attitude to their tenants, spending large amounts of money for famine relief last century when the potato crops failed. In 1705, which was a bad year, MacLeod actually cancelled 'eases' owing by his Harris tenants, as a generous gesture. In 1712, when disaster overtook the natives of now-deserted St Kilda, MacLeod provided them with a new boat and allowed them a two-year delay in payment of their rents to help them get back on their feet again. The MacLeods retained Harris until the end of the eighteenth century, when it was purchased by a cadet of the family, who had made a fortune in East Asia. Much of this was ploughed into his Harris estate in far-reaching schemes, such as the development of fishing. But the schemes were never successful, and in 1834 the estate passed to the Earl of Dunmore, who had no Hebridean connections.

The Dunmores, however, proved to be more than mere landlords. The Countess of Dunmore became interested in the quality of cloth being woven by the women of Harris and she sent some lengths of the cloth, Harris Tweed as it was known, to London. Immediately a market was created and, though nowadays much of the Harris Tweed is woven in the homes of Lewis weavers, it was the enterprise of the Dunmores which began an industry which has become such a social sheet-anchor in the economy of the islands.

One of the most interesting sites in Harris, and indeed in the whole of the Western Isles, is St Clement's church at Rodel, in the south-east corner of the island. It was built early in the sixteenth century by the MacLeods of Harris on the site of a much earlier structure and features an impressive tower, on the walls of which are a number of stone-carved panels. The interior of the building would be rather stark were it not for one of the most impressive tombs to be found in Scotland. Set into the

St Clement's church, Rodel, in Harris

south wall of the choir is the remarkable memorial to Alexander MacLeod of Harris, who died in 1547. Prepared for himself 19 years before his death, the arched tomb is elaborately wrought, with sculptured panels and the recumbent effigy of a Highland warrior chief of the period, with animals guarding the head and feet. Set in the floor of the choir are four grave slabs, each displaying a sword and other ornamentation of the sixteenth century.

Also buried in St Clement's of Rodel is Mary MacLeod, unusual in the fact that she rose to the highest rank of Gaelic bards in the seventeenth century. She was employed as governess to the young MacLeods at Dunvegan Castle. She was the first to compose what might be called the 'court song', in simple words and in the strophic verse-form of rhythm and assonance, which was a feature of the Gaelic poetry composed at that time. She is reputed to have asked to be buried face down so that she would always be in contact with the earth of her native Harris.

Memorials of a rather different kind, and much less appealing, can still be seen at Leverburgh, originally called Obbe, a small straggling township on the south shore of Harris facing the Sound of Harris. These are the sad remains of the schemes of Lord Leverhulme, once the king of Sunlight Soap. He came into the Western Isles scene by buying Lewis from the descendants of Sir James Matheson after World War I. Not one to let his money lie in banks and gain interest, Leverhulme's burning energy led him to lay schemes for the industrialization of Lewis, based on the potential of the fishing wealth in the waters round the Hebrides. But he was the right man in the right place at the wrong time, for what was uppermost in the minds of the folk of Lewis was the need to get land for crofts. No matter how much Leverhulme tried to persuade these landless men that there was a better future in his industrial schemes, he failed eventually to persuade them of the attraction of secure jobs in an industrialized society. When his Lewis plans came to nothing, he sold Lewis and bought the south Harris estate. Obbe, renamed Leverburgh, became the focal point for his schemes. He built a large pier, huge kippering sheds, houses for the workers, roads and lighthouses, and blasted away underwater rocks which hindered free access to the harbour. By 1924 the bulk of this work was completed but when he died the following year, his business successors decided to close down the embryo industrial complex and realise its assets. The harbour works alone cost £250,000; they were sold for £5000 to a demolition company. Mute witnesses to Leverhulme can still be seen in Leverburgh.

Apart from the numerous islands in the Sound of Harris, Harris also has three offshore islands. Taransay and Scarp are now deserted; the latter saw its indigenous population leave its shore in 1971. However, Scalpay, lying at the mouth of East Loch Tarbert, is a long way from becoming yet another mute reminder of the problems of island living. Its present population is around 450. But small island living demands commitment and determination. From an agricultural point of view the crofts yield little more than the normal subsistence levels. The riches of the sea have, however, not been ignored. Scalpay men have, in fact, developed their fishing skills to a level that has put them as rivals to Eriskay, another island which has had to look to the sea for its survival. At one time the Scalpay community boasted the largest number of full-time fishermen of any community in the Western Isles, employed on no fewer than 38 fishing boats. Not only that but they have developed landing facilities through their own Scalpay Harbour Association. Native enterprise is also demonstrated in a small ship-owning firm, whose vessels carry freight to the islands, to mainland Scotland and even to the Continent. This spirit of independence and faith in their future has marked the Scalpay islanders out as one of the exceptions to the rule.

Tarbert

With a population of around 400, Tarbert acts as the focal point for Harris, enhanced with its role as the main ferry terminal between Skye and Lochmaddy. Situated at the head of East Loch Tarbert, it lies in a comfortable and sheltered location. Though the village is mainly linear in pattern, its streets take full advantage of the hilly nature of the terrain and dive and rise in a manner which adds no little interest to a walk around Tarbert. Visitors arriving at Tarbert will see their first aspect of the nature of the east Harris landscape: hills with numerous exposed patches of native rock, resisting the weathering of the elements and lending a delightful contrast to the gardens and trees which have somehow survived the stunting effects of the southwesterly gales, which are common in winter months. The pier facilities have undergone something of a transformation to accommodate the new roll-on/roll-off car ferry *Hebridean Isles*. Before she came on the scene in 1986 cars had a rather traumatic route to get from the bowels of the old *Hebrides* and on to the pier.

North Uist

Looking down on the landscape of North Uist from the top of Eaval, one is immediately struck by the amount of water held fast by the moorland. Large and small lochs are scattered generously as far as the eye can see. Tidal lochs and inlets lend their own distinctive patterns on the coast, and tidal flats offer a kaleidoscope of colour; blues, greens and turquoise, as the sea ebbs and flows in its own due time. Relief of the general flatness on the island is given by Eaval and a similar group of hills, the Lees, a little to the north. It is to the west, however, that one must look to see the sharp contrast offered by the machair; here is where much of the population live in crofting townships and here is where much of the scenic interest of North Uist lies.

The northern side of North Uist looks on to the Sound of Harris, once described as a 'chaos of rocks and islands'. Some are mere pinpoints of rock; others once supported populations and today only Berneray still manages to keep its folk content and happy despite the odds. One of these islands has its own place in the history books: Hermetray. It was on this island that 'The Company of the General Fishing of Great Britain and Ireland', promoted by Charles I, built a curing station and store houses for fish caught in Minch waters. The enterprise met with no little justified opposition from the islanders on North Uist, who were quite excluded from the 'pickings'. Indeed, it was this fact that forced the Company to choose small and comparatively remote islands on which to establish their stations.

If the north coast is dominated by islands, then so is the western side of North Uist. Here lie the tidal islands of Kirkibost and Baleshare, the latter

Broch at Dun Carloway, Lewis. Its fine state of preservation and spectacular site are a magnet for visitors (over)

sporting the shell-sand beach of Traigh Iar, which is a favourite breeding ground for a large number of waders, with significant colonies of arctic and little terns. These islands, largely based on sand, are constantly changing their shape and features as the wind cuts deeply serrated blowouts. The 1837 Statistical Account said of Kirkibost: 'This island was at one time of considerable value. It is composed of the fine sand already described and, being exposed to the western gales, a great part of it was literally blown away and the sea now occupies fields which formerly produced fine crops of bear or barley'.

Some miles to the north-west, the small island of Vallay is tucked into a wide but shallow sand bight. To the west of Vallay lie the remains of a forest of trees, now covered by the sea at high tide, which offer proof that the Western Isles were once covered by woodland and scrub. This evidence of an ancient past is commemorated in a small bay called Bagh nan Craobhag (Bay of Small Trees). About thirty years ago investigations were carried out on the possibility of machair-type sand being suitable for growing bulbs. Sporadic interest then led to some small-scale experiments which met with varied success; on the whole, however, it was generally agreed that there was a potential for this area of North Uist to become a *Little Holland*. More experimental planting was carried out, which proved that the bulbs grew well in the soil and climate of the islands. Gradually the project grew in size until the stage was reached at which, given expert management, a large-scale undertaking could yield significant profits. A Dutch firm was commissioned to look at the possibility of reclaiming 1500 acres of the tidal calcareous sands known as the Vallay Strand. In 1969 the Dutch reported the technical feasibility of the scheme – but there it ended, for the Scottish Office refused to come up with the capital. One wonders, twenty years on, about the boost in employment, to say nothing of extra cash for an unusual crofting crop, had such a significant scheme been allowed to go ahead.

Some five miles off the North Uist coast, lying in the stream of Atlantic waters, are the Monach Isles, a group of five islands, three of which are joined together at low water by exposed shallow sandy beaches. Less than 50 foot above sea level, these islands have had a history of human settlement going back before AD 1000. One of the earliest references to them concerns the establishment of a nunnery attached to Iona, the mother church, on one of the islands, Ceann Ear. On another island a monastery for monks was built, with a specific duty detailed for the monks: to maintain a light as a navigational aid to mariners. Long after that monastery fell into ruins a lighthouse (now deserted) was erected in 1864 on the same site to carry on the tradition. The Monach Isles once supported as many as a hundred people; by 1764 the population had fallen to 70. About 1810 the islands were finally deserted, the result of a complete failure of the soil, when over-grazing exposed large areas of sand, winds then wreaking havoc with the turf until all the islands were covered with worthless sand. Later an effort was made to anchor the sand by planting marram grass; this was successful enough to allow a new population to live on the islands so that, by 1891, 135 people found the means to exist. The islands were finally deserted for good in 1942, to enter the catalogue of so many of the small islands of the Outer Hebrides which once supported a population and are now lonely memorials to the difficulties of island living.

Despite the often depressing monotony of the moors and boglands of the central areas of North Uist, an environment which is of little use other than as very rough grazing for sheep, the island offers a significant environment for a very rich and varied wildlife. North Uist is becoming increasingly known as a bird-watching centre, with a kaleidoscope of habitats ranging from the rich coastal grassland, coastal and moorland marshes, beaches, tidal inlets and peaty brown freshwater lochs. Both migratory and breeding species of birds enjoy North Uist, as do animals ranging from red deer to seals, the latter breeding on the Monach Isles in large numbers. The Balranald Bird Reserve, maintained by the Royal Society for the Protection of Birds, is centred on a fine surviving marshland which lies between the townships of Hougharry and Balranald.

Lochmaddy

Lochmaddy, the 'capital' of the island, sits at the end of a broad sea inlet in a kind of grand isolation – for it is really the only settlement of any size on the eastern side of North Uist, and is thus some distance away from the more populous west coast townships. One of the earliest mentions of Lochmaddy was made in documentary records of 1616, in a complaint of piracy and murder in Lewis which made a special mention of 'Lochmaldie on the coast of Uist' as being a rendezvous for pirates. Certainly the maze of small islands on the coast hereabouts made the area a safe hiding place for marauding ships intent on intercepting other vessels, perhaps carrying large supplies of wine and fine goods to the clan chiefs of the time. As with most of the major settlements in the Western Isles, Lochmaddy saw its rise in importance as a major fishing station during last century when the herring fishing industry was at its height. After that industry declined, in the years following World War I, Lochmaddy settled down to being a small commercial port for the many passenger and cargo boats which once plied the Minch waters. A boost to its status was given when the direct link with Uig in Skye was established, which also links it with Tarbert in Harris. With the advent of roll-on/roll-off ferry facilities, Lochmaddy now experiences a fair amount of port activities connected with the army presence on the islands.

Benbecula

Though Benbecula (Gaelic: Mountain of the Fords) has always been something of a stepping stone between North and South Uist, it is an

75

Lochmaddy quay is a focal point for North Uist's residents

island in its own right with as rich a prehistory and recorded history as its larger neighbours. Benbecula displays the same topographical features as other Outer Hebridean islands: smooth-lying sandy beaches on the western side and deeply indented sea lochs, with attendant rock islands, on the east. It was once said of Benbecula: 'The sea here is all islands, and the land all lakes. That which is not rock is sand; and that which is not mud is bog; that which is not bog is lake; that which is not lake is sea; and the whole is a labyrinth of islands, peninsulas, promontories, bays and channels.'

Despite its Gaelic name, Benbecula's only mountain is named Rueval, betraying its Norse origin. It is, in fact, a rather rounded hill with grassy and heather slopes but which affords a splendid view from its assuming summit. While Rueval gives some physical prominence to the island, Benbecula has another significance in the Western Isles, for here is located the sub-centre for local government. Not only that, the airport provides the island with a sense of purpose and no little importance. Indeed, the presence in Balivanich, the main township, of the Army

Rocket Range administrative headquarters has given the island a magnetic pull towards which much economic activity has gravitated, creating an uneasy syncopation in its social equilibrium with the neighbouring islands.

Even so, Benbecula seems to enjoy its central position, for in the past it has tended to be neglected. One guidebook to the Western Isles, published some years ago, scarcely mentioned the island in its prosy eloquence extolling the delights of the Outer Hebrides. Things are much better now. Benbecula's relative isolation came to an end with the building of the South Ford causeway in 1942 and the North Uist causeway in 1963. Before that access north and south was by means of crossing sandy fords at low tides, on foot or on horseback. While these two dates are significant, it was in the late 1950s that the island became the focus of great attention, with the announcement that a rocket-testing range was to be established on South Uist and Benbecula was to become the location of a large military presence. The airport at Balivanich had, in fact, been set up as a military facility during World War II and now it was to assume a new role in the chain of Britain's coastal defences based on the North Atlantic.

Those factions concerned about the erosion of an existing all-Gaelic community, with consequences for the cultural and linguistic aspects of the island, were vociferous in their accusations that the army on Benbecula would be a polluting element in the culture. Others, however, suggested that the military presence would be welcome on economic grounds. One writer, Sir Compton MacKenzie, saw in the situation material for a book which was subsequently made into a film, 'Rockets Galore', an echo of his famous book and film 'Whisky Galore', filmed on location in Barra. In the event, the fears that the underlying cultural links would be severed by the presence of a monoglot English community have not been realized, though there has been some erosion of the native language and culture. The islanders, in fact, have kept a firm hold on their traditions and are a calm pool of social values in a whirlwind of imported militarism.

These traditions are important, for the confidence of any community in its future must be based on its past experience, and how the people have weathered both fair winds and bad. An example of how strong the hold has been on the cultural facets of Gaelic was evidenced in 1948 when a Benbecula crofter, Angus MacMillan, was found to be a treasurehouse of folklore and stories. His memory was committed to the tape recorder and the result was some 500 recordings, with one item lasting for a full four hours, amounting to nearly 5000 large manuscript pages of stories. The prodigious memory and knowledge of this old man, who died in 1954, was something of a legend in the field of international folklore studies, as he could neither read nor write. A description of him is given by Sean O Suilleabhain, who collected so much of Angus' material:

Harbour improvements under the Integrated Development Programme, Kallin, Grimsay, Benbecula

Next day he (Calum MacLean) took me to meet a man whome he described as the greatest storyteller he had met thus far, Angus (Barrach) MacMillan of Griminish. Two years previously, Calum had heard of Angus's prowess as a narrator of tales and had already recorded a large number of them from him when I met him. For myself, going to meet such a man was like making a pilgrimage. Angus was 72 years of age at that time; powerfully built and over six feet tall, he was wearing a blue 'gansey' as he sat by the fire. As I had only a smattering of Scots Gaelic, as spoken, I had difficulty in understanding the long tale which Calum recorded from him for my benefit. When the long narration was over, Calum, as was his wont, replayed on the Ediphone machine the concluding sentences of the tale in order to check the clarity of the recording and Angus, having heard his own voice again, gave his usual verdict (as Calum later told me) by uttering the only word of English which he knew: 'Perfection.'

Angus MacMillan was, of course, one of the last of the truly great storytellers, deriving his knowledge from his father and continuing a long and worthy family tradition. Having said that, it is heartening to know that members of the following generation of tradition-bearers in Benbecula are well capable of taking Gaelic and its culture into the 21st century.

Balivanich
Since the advent of the military presence in the Western Isles, Balivanich has been transformed from a small crofting township into a major social and economic centre for Benbecula. Despite its advantageous situation looking towards the waters of the Atlantic and the sandy shallows of Beul an Toim, the planners of both Local Authority and military housing facilities have not seen fit to exploit the obvious scenic attractions. The result is a rather depressing vista, which the general flatness of the area does nothing to relieve. Evidence of two cultures is seen in the names of roads: Winfield Way contrasts incongruously with Rathad Mhic Eoin and Druim na h-Airde.

Balivanich is derived from Baile Mhanich, the town of the monks, a reminder that the first settlement here was associated with a monastery erected with grants of lands from the old Lordship of the Isles. Its strategic importance during World War II led to the building of the airport, since when the development of the facility made it a focal point for military activities. Now, large military planes contrast sharply with the smaller planes of the inter-island routes operated by Loganair.

A faint echo of the past can be seen in the ruined little chapel which stands only a few hundred yards from the entrance to the army headquarters and was once dedicated to St Columba, whose message was peace to all men. Because of its relative isolation, the old monastery survived the attention of Reformation zealots and was functioning in the seventeenth century. Martin Martin, one of the earliest travel writers in the Western Isles, wrote up his experiences in a book published in the 1690s, in which he makes a reference to an echo of the former Balivanich monastery:

> I remember I have seen an old lay Capuchin here, call'd in the Language Brahir-bocht, that is Poor Brother; which is literally true, for he answers this Character, having nothing but what is given him: He holds himself fully satisfied with Food and Rayment, and lives in as great Simplicity as any of his Order; his diet is very mean, and he drinks only fair Water: his Habit is no less mortifying than that of his Brethren elsewhere; he wears a short Coat, which comes no further than his Middle, with narrow sleeves like a Waistcoat; he wears a Plad above it girt about the Middle, which reaches to his Knee: the Plad is fasten'd on his Breast with a Wooden Pin, his Kneck bare, and his Feet often so too: he wears a Hat for ornament, and the String about it is a bit of Fisher's Line made of Horse-hair. This Plad he wears instead of a Gown worn

South Ford Causeway connects North Uist with Benbecula

by those of his Order in other countries. I told him he wanted a flaxen Girdle that men of his Order usually wear; he answered me that he wore a Leather one, which was the same thing. Upon the matter, if he is spoken to when at Meat, he answeres again; which is contrary to the Custom of his Order. This poor Man frequently diverts himself with Angling of Trouts; he lies upon Straw, and had no Bell (as others have) to call him to his Devotion, but only his Conscience, as he told me.

About a century later a priest returned from the Scots College in Rome to his native Uist and built a thatched chapel in Balivanich, which could accommodate some 400 people. By 1850 this building was reported as falling into a ruin.

Apart from the military presence, Balivanich acts as a sub-centre for Local Authority services for the southern isles, a role which has been criticised for its 'black hole' effect, which tends to draw in to itself much of the social and economic activity of the island, which would be better dispersed.

South Uist

Next to Lewis, South Uist is the largest mass in the Long Island chain. Some 22 miles long, and from six to eight miles wide, virtually all its population lives on the western side. The eastern side and central area is wild with boggy moorland that rises to meet a long spine of high hills which run the length of the island. Only Lochboisdale, the ferry terminal township, breaks the impression of coastal desolation as one sails down the Minch. The island is deeply indented by three long sea lochs on the Minch side, which effectively divide South Uist into three parts: Loch Eynort, Loch Skiport and Loch Boisdale. Indeed, Loch Skiport almost makes an island of the northern part where it just fails to reach Loch Bee to the northwest. Ben Mhor reaches a respectable height of 2034 foot, with other attendant peaks, such as Hecla (1988 foot), lending a welcome break on the horizon. A number of short-run rivers drain the land into the various lochs which act as sediment traps to offer some meagre sustenance for brown trout.

The road which runs north-south through the length of the eastern side of the island acts as an artery with laterals to join together all the crofting townships on South Uist. The road runs by Loch Bee, the largest inland mass of water, and then skirts the western shores of Loch Druidibeg, a National Nature Reserve which contains the most important native Greylag Goose breeding ground in the British Isles. The Reserve extends from the western foothills of Hecla, across a glacially-scoured platform to a coastal machair and complex of sand dunes.

The Reserve is largely owned by the Nature Conservancy, with a resident Warden who oversees the 4000 acres and to whom visitors should apply for information about access and what to see. Near the township of Milton can be seen the remains of the house where Flora MacDonald was born. She entered the history books, to say nothing of popular imagination, when she became involved in plans to take the dejected Prince Charles Edward off the Hebrides across the Minch to Skye and, subsequently, escape to France after the Battle of Culloden in April 1746.

The official end of the main road is at Pollachar at the southern tip of the island, from where a side road goes on to Ludac, the ferry terminal for the island of Eriskay. From Ludac one can see the many small islands in the Sound of Barra beckoning one to visit Barra on the horizon.

But just to keep to the main road would be to miss the real flavour of South Uist. There are ample opportunities to take the many minor roads which link the numerous crofting townships situated on the extensive machair, dotted with lochs, many of which are covered by water lilies. Perhaps the most important target for any sightseeing visit is Ormacleit Castle, now a rather muted ruin but still exuding that sense of the past which sets the imagination running off at interesting tangents. The old church at Bornish was originally built because it was at the centre of the

Kilbride, South Uist

island's population at one time. Now that centre has shifted farther south and the chapel is today a quiet monument to its own past. Built of natural local stone its interior is rather bare but, in compensation, it provides an appropriate atmosphere for reflection and contemplation. If Bornish is muted, the same cannot be said for the new church at Garrynamonie, just south of Daliburgh. This is a modern expression of confidence in the future of the Catholic faith in the southern isles, with mosaic murals, an interesting window, and Stations of the Cross.

Of more traditional design is St Peter's at Daliburgh, a handsome building of substantial proportions which reflects its importance in the life of the South Uist folk. Another expression of faith is to be seen on the side of Rueval, about four miles south of Carnan at the northern end of the island. This is the tall slender statue of Our Lady of the Isles with the Holy Child. The statue overlooks the army's rocket firing range at Iochdar, in some kind of mutual tolerance of each other's meaning for our times.

Lochboisdale

With the growth of Daliburgh as a population centre, Lochboisdale, the real 'capital' of South Uist, has lost much of its status. Even so, it is still a focal point in island life, acting now as the ferry terminal. In its heyday last century, when the herring was king and the fishing industry dominated all economic life in the Western Isles, Lochboisdale was a major herring port and witnessed scenes of industrious activity that crammed to the brim its little streets with fishermen, salesmen, fish curers and herring girls. Today there is only the sense of a quiet reflection of its former boom days. The car ferry links the town with Castlebay, in Barra, and Oban on the Argyll mainland. The importance of Lochboisdale as a commercial port was reduced considerably when the Uig to Lochmaddy direct link was established across the Minch.

Barra

Barra is the most westerly inhabited island in Great Britain. It lies, with its satellite companion Vatersay, at the southern end of the Long Island chain, a position which, before the Western Isles became a most-purpose Local Authority, tended to make it fall last in the queue for whatever meagre pickings were to be had after the other islands had had their share of public services. Since the inception of Comhairle nan Eilean, in 1974, Barra has seen a vast improvement in these provisions which may be, directly or indirectly, the reason why the population has increased by about 25 per cent in the last 15 years or so, the result of a net in-migration of folk, in contrast to marked declines in previous decades. For instance, between 1951 and 1971 the population actually fell by 43 per cent. Today, the island's age structure is quite healthy; proportionately, there are more young, and working age, and less elderly persons than in 1971.

From a distance, from the seaward approach, Barra tends to give the impression of being bleak and inhospitable. In fact, closer inspection reveals a more than interesting kaleidoscope of greens, browns and greys which contrast with the blues and greens of the vast expanses of sand, particularly to the north and north west. The highest peak is Heaval (1260 ft) which affords an excellent viewpoint from which to see the whole island, to say nothing of glimpses of the 1000 ft cliffs of far-off St Kilda and the peaks of mainland Scotland. In springtime and summer, the machairs are a carpet of wild flowers, all taking advantage of the salt-tasting shell sand which reduces the sharpness of the acidic peat which covers most of the island.

Nask, Barra. A hillside of sheep and stones

All the island townships are served by a circular road, with minor roads leading to those communities off the beaten track, including the narrow promontory at the north of the island which is joined to the main island mass by a vast cockle-shell beach. This latter feature also serves as the island's airstrip, possibly the only airport in the British Isles where flights are timed to coincide with the ebbing tide. During the hungry years of last century, when the island folk were placed under great duress by the new owners, this cockle strand was a life-saver, though, at times, even that source of simple food was denied them. Today, the shells are turned into a roughcasting material for buildings, which is durable and inexpensive, offering a useful pocket of employment in an island which has an inevitably narrow job spectrum.

Only a small part of the island is cultivated by crofting. However, there are a number of places where, in the past, intensive cultivation took place; for example, in a rich alluvial valley at Borve on the western side of the island. There are also other signs of a past use of land in the form of 'lazybeds', which is the common, but misused, name for the man-made ridges of earth fertilized with seaweed, which were used for growing potatoes in the days when the population of Barra was much higher than it is today and crofting was the main means of life-support.

Castlebay

The main settlement on Barra is Castlebay, sitting snugly in the crook of a sheltered bay. Those who have seen the film 'Whisky Galore', based on the book by Compton MacKenzie who lived for a few years on the island, may remember some of the street scenes. Main Street is lined with substantial buildings facing the bay. The centre of activity, however, is at the pier where the car ferry from Lochboisdale and Oban, some 85 miles distant on the Scottish mainland, berths. Almost a stone's throw away is Kisimul Castle, which lends an extra dimension of interest to any photograph.

Castlebay came into its own during last century when it was one of the main herring stations of the west coast of Scotland. In fact, it assumed such importance that, at one time, it rivalled Stornoway. It is on record that occasions occurred when Castlebay's spacious harbour could not contain all the fishing boats requiring berthing space, and boats had to land their catches on nearby Vatersay. In 1886, no fewer than 400 fishing boats congregated in the bay from May to the end of June. At the height of the fishing season some 2000 persons were employed on the island, though not all were islanders. After the herring fishing declined, Castlebay slumped into a twilight haze, to become a delight for visitors from the many and frequent passenger ferries which plied the Minch waters before World War II. Something of a revival occurred in 1970, when the port received a welcome boost from a steady stream of klondykers (factory ships) from Europe, eager to buy up Minch-caught herring for subsequent processing in foreign ports. But this trade was short-lived and, though Castlebay still serves a small local fishing fleet, these days are but an echo of the heady times of the past.

Recent efforts by the island to become a tourist attraction, boosted in no small way by the Feis Bharraidh, have given Castlebay a cosmopolitan look in the summer months, giving welcome seasonable employment to many islanders.

Vatersay

This island is the most southerly inhabited island of the Western Isles. Lying just across from Barra, it is a curious double-headed mass, each head joined together by a low isthmus of sandy hillocks. The population of just over 100 faces an uncertain future, with some determination not to be added to the list of depopulated Hebridean islands which includes

Southward-facing statue atop Heaval, near Castlebay, Barra

some of its own satellite companions: Sandray, Pabbay, Mingulay and Berneray – the most southerly island in the Long Island chain. Four crofting townships provide the basis for the island's economy, though one wonders what might be needed to bring Vatersay to the level of fertility indicated in a report dated 1886, which said that the island supported 1200 cattle and 400 sheep. Much of the population is derived from the original 'Vatersay Raiders', who occupied the island at the turn of the century when it was used as a farm by the owner of Barra. The islesfolk are very much dependent on the services enjoyed by Barra, which include medical attention. Even so, the islanders have demonstrated their community spirit with the formation of Vatersay Co-operative, which pools resources, initiative and enterprise. A current controversy rages over a proposed causeway or bridge to link the island with Barra, to act as a much-needed lifeline.

A granite memorial on the island is a poignant reminder of the last century, when Highland folk were forced to leave their native shores. It commemorates the wreck of the *Annie Jane*, an emigrant ship bound for America out of Liverpool. The passengers were 'redemptioners' – the term given to emigrants who booked passages that were to be paid for by instalments out of their earnings when they arrived on the other side of the Atlantic. Because of the bad weather, the ship had to return twice to Liverpool. On the third attempt some headway was made, but gales swept the *Annie Jane* northwards to find herself near Vatersay where she went aground and broke up. More than 350 people were drowned in a tragedy made all the more telling by the fact that some were from the Western Isles, hoping to find a new life in the New World but, instead, finding an eternal rest on their own native shores.

Eriskay

Known to most people through the song, 'Eriskay Love Lilt', Eriskay lies off the south-eastern tip of South Uist. About 200 people enjoy the island's environment. The economy is based on crofting and fishing, the latter brought to a pitch of perfection by men who realized only too well that crofting could offer only subsistence living. A Report of 1903 stated: 'Eriskay is inhabited by a fishing community. Formerly most of the able-bodied men were in use to go to the East Coast of Scotland fishing, but they have not been going in large numbers in recent years. The explanation is that the East Coast fishing has often proved uncertain, and that, with the better class of boats now owned by the people, they do fully better at home, that is by fishing in the neighbourhood of their own island and also in the West Highland lochs . . .'

That initial taste for fishing has lasted for some eight decades and created a breed of fishermen whose skills are rarely surpassed, even by that other fishing-based island, Scalpay.

In 1941, a 12,000 ton cargo ship ran aground on Calvay, a small island at the eastern inlet to the Sound of Eriskay. The cargo included 24,000 cases of whisky bound for the American market. The crew were taken off safely and with them came news of the nature of the ship's lading. In no time at all a rescue attempt was mounted by the islanders, who managed to take off enough cases of the amber liquid to see them through the dark and dreary days of World War II. The incident was too tempting for author Compton MacKenzie, who wrote a book which was subsequently filmed and widely acclaimed. In reality, some of the 'rescuers' went up to the Sheriff at Lochmaddy for offences against the excise laws and were sentenced to two months' imprisonment. No doubt they thought it was worth it.

Darning Harris Tweed at Shawbost, Lewis. The outworking side of the industry remains an important part of the island economy (over)

Castlebay

Berneray

This island lies at the western end of the Sound of Harris and supports a crofting population of about 130. Most of the folk live in the south-east corner of the island, which is connected to North Uist and Harris by a small ferry. As exists in other small islands, like Vatersay and Eriskay, there is a spirit of self-determination which has sliced through piles of red tape to achieve some of the trappings of life which more well-endowed communities take for granted. Three township roads have been built and a new harbour is to be constructed with Common Market funds. The island's car ferry came as the result of a continuous programme of articulated agitation, as did the ten new Local Authority houses. It is reckoned that some £3 million has been spent in the last ten years to provide adequate facilities for the islanders.

The car ferry Claymore *arriving at Castlebay*

If that sum might tend to catch one's breath, it should be remembered that decades of downright neglect of Berneray and similar island communities have done untold harm to the prospects and potential inherent in the islands. That same neglect was instrumental in reducing the Berneray population from over 500 in 1901 to what it is today and, in another statistic, deterring the population from seeking its own salvation in its young folk: in 1865 there were three schools on the island, including a 'Female Industrial School' in which domestic and potential commercial skills were taught to girls.

Berneray Community Council meets monthly to discuss the current problems and identifies possible solutions. And, while nothing is solved overnight, at least the community's ability to articulate and argue cogent cases for their requirements goes a long way to ensuring that the future, while it remains ever uneasy, at least may have a silver lining to it.

Fishing is a mainstay of the economy on Berneray

5. The Islanders

There are two types of islanders. The first category includes those who live on a small island, often within a stone's throw of a mainland so well-endowed with the trappings of civilization that their island lifestyle, while not exactly a personal indulgence, tends to be followed in the knowledge that a safety net is available at all times of need.

The second category includes those who live in island groupings, whose lifestyle has to be hammered out and tempered in a fire of community interdependence. Life in this case has a keen knife edge to it, which itself engenders a different kind of philosophy of living. Characters are moulded from a progression of difficulties created by geographical distance and relative, though often real, remoteness from the services which urban communities too often take for granted. In addition, cultural and social norms tend to be strong and based on the accretions built up by previous generations in the times of their own contemporary historical experiences. Of the four main island groupings in the north and west of Scotland, three, Orkney, Shetland and the Western Isles, display some of the characteristics described above. The fourth grouping, the Inner Hebrides, while there may be residual elements still extant, has seen a decline in the homogeneity which once identified their inhabitants with those in the first three groupings. This is not to say that life in the Inner Hebrides is a bed of roses, but to indicate that their more immediate accessibility to the Scottish mainland has made it easier for dilutive influences to make a greater impact. The Gaelic cultural domain is the one which has suffered most. Once such a cohesive element disappears from a community, other factors tend to assume a greater corrosive role – social structures fail and the spirit of self-determination weakens.

The folk of the Western Isles have often been described as being 'a lively people'. Yet, it was not always a description used about them. One recalls the report which eventually excited the Fife Adventurers into mounting an expedition to Lewis, in which the folk of Lewis were described as wicked and barbarous. In later times, and in particular when the unfortunate mist of 'Celtic Twilight' descended on the islands at the turn of this century, the islesfolk were looked upon as curious archaic characters, ever indulging in whimsy and folklore, while in reality they were suffering from social and economic deprivation. Popular images of

A lamb sale in Arnol, Lewis

the islanders were portrayed in films, such as *The Maggie*, *Whisky Galore*, *Bridal Path* and others which tended to confirm outsiders in their mistaken belief that island living was one great time of indulgence in which the long days were whiled away in capers.

There were other descriptions, too, which were nearer the truth. 'The inhabitants of the Western Scottish Isles or Hebrides are all so much accustomed to a seafaring life, and retain so much of the native heroism of ancient Highlanders, that almost everything great and successful may be hoped from their gallantry during the war'. While that statement was to be echoed, in its sentiment, during the many wartime periods which Great Britain found itself enduring, it in fact dates from 1801 and appears in the *Naval Chronicle* written at a time when Britain was at war with the Northern Confederacy of Russia, Sweden and Norway. This record of the islesmen in wartime was highlighted in the two World Wars, in which the Western Isles suffered losses which were twice as heavy, in proportion to their population, as the rest of Britain. In the Great War of 1914–18, out of a total population of nearly 30,000, Lewis alone had over 6000 men on active service, of whom more than 1100 lost their lives.

Two men typify the contribution to the war arenas by islanders. 'His appearance marks him well and without a shadow of doubt as a seafarer. His handsome, rugged Scottish face and great powerful hands have been tanned by hot tropical suns and salt sea breezes, and his incredibly bright, light blue eyes are of the kind only ever found in men who have spent a lifetime gazing at a distant horizon where the green ocean and the blue sky meet.' This was said by the late radio entertainer Wilfred Pickles of Bos'n Kenneth Stewart, who was the model for the Merchant Navy Memorial on Tower Hill, London. Born at Tong, just outside Stornoway, he joined the Merchant Service at £6 per month, at a time when crews slept on bags filled with straw in a packed fo'c'sle and had their water supply locked up from 1800 hrs until 0530 hrs the next day. He had an outstanding career in the Merchant Service and in both World Wars; during the latter he carried out a brave rescue attempt, saving three men from an accident on the *Sussex* in Sydney Harbour, Australia, for which he was awarded the Royal Humane Society Certificate for Lifesaving and received the BEM in later life.

One story of bravery concerns an 18-year-old lad from Lochs, Lewis. He was one of the crew of the *Arlington Court*, working as a deck boy when she was sunk far out in the Atlantic. As the newspaper 'The Scotsman' reported at the time: 'Today's story of Malcolm Morrison's remarkable feat of seamanship and endurance after his ship had been torpedoed over 300 miles in the Atlantic must have been heard with a thrill of pride far beyond his native village. This 18-year-old youth's action in taking charge of a water-logged lifeboat for six days and steering it to safety ranks with the great stories of heroism at sea. Morrison comes from the island with a notable tradition of naval service . . . and his feat supports the claim that Lewis seamen are above the average intelligence, reliability and initiative. Of the six men in the lifeboat he was the only one who knew how to set a sail, and he gave further proof of his seamanship when he made a course with the aid of a small compass. When the men were landed from the rescue ship, he refused to be treated as an invalid, surely a final stamp of heroism.'

Many Scots played important roles in European history and rose to the highest positions their adopted countries could offer. One man whose forebears came from South Uist was the French Duke of Tarentum, or Marshall MacDonald. He was promoted to Marshall on the field of the Battle of Wagram by Napoleon in 1809 and afterwards created a Duke and Peer of France. His father was Neil MacEachen, born in the township of Howbeg in South Uist. Neil left his native island in his early teens to become a student priest, but left that calling to become a serving French soldier employed as a Jacobite under-cover agent. He accompanied Prince Charles Edward Stuart after the Battle of Culloden in 1746 while the Prince's party scoured the Western Isles for a ship to take them to safety. In later life the Marshall paid a visit to South Uist to see the island of his father and, on leaving, took back a box of soil to France, so that he could be buried with a tangible witness to his ancestry, 'In a corner of a foreign field . . .'.

A small plaque on the wall of Martin's Memorial Church in Stornoway marks the site of the birthplace of Sir Alexander MacKenzie. Born in 1764 MacKenzie grew up in the town which was then little more than a prosperous village, being the centre of both fishing and trading activity. Not yet into his teens his family emigrated to America and then to Canada, where MacKenzie went into service as a clerk to a firm of Montreal fur traders. By the time he was twenty he had acquired a great deal of knowledge about the fur trade and was sent on successful missions to make contacts with Indians in the back country of Canada. These so impressed his employers that he was made a partner. He then developed into a unique character for his times, which were clouded by the greed for profit derived from animal furs. It is MacKenzie's distinction that he turned this single-minded quest for commercial profit into a broader intention – having the benefit of his adopted country in view – and that his pursuit of his objectives, at every level of activity, was so free of deceit, cruelty and aggression.

His main interest was to discover the North-West Passage between the Atlantic and the Pacific and his explorations of the great wilderness of northern Canada have gone down in the annals of enduring feats. He is remembered today in the MacKenzie River, the lowest reaches of which gave MacKenzie his road to the Arctic. His fort at Lake Athabasca was, by coincidence, on exactly the same latitude as his native Stornoway.

Another MacKenzie from Stornoway looked to the Far East for his fame and fortune. He was Colin, who became Surveyor-General of India. Born in 1754 in Carn House on South Beach Street, on the site which is now a garden beside the Town Hall, he went to Madras as a cadet in the Engineer Corps of the East India Company. He followed a career of high professional distinction and was marked out as being different to his colleagues whose motives were always profit. This 'difference' took the form of an unusually intense interest in the languages and traditions of India. During his lifetime he amassed a vast collection of Indian antiques, including manuscripts, which is still intact and an important source of reference for scholars. MacKenzie, unlike many of the famous names associated with the era of the East India Company, is still remembered with great respect today, two centuries after his sojourn in India. One of the mutineers of the famous ship *Bounty* was a James Morrison from Stornoway. Condemned to death but later reprieved, he was in Australia in the year that Australian history is said to have begun. He wrote extensively of life in Polynesia and provided the first missionaries to Tahiti with the vocabulary which made their work possible.

For all that the islanders have bred men and women who have had the stamina and courage to stay at home to struggle with their destinies on the home front, there have also been others who have looked beyond their

The Reverend MacLeod and elders, Gravir, Lewis

island horizons to seek out careers of a different kind. And, as so often happens, they make their mark on other societies often greatly exceeding the size of the community they left behind. And, as frequently, their descendants carve significant niches in the histories of the countries adopted by their parents. Minds and spirits bred in the Highlands and Islands have a peculiar potential for development not always apparent on native soil but sometimes fully realized in alien surroundings and conditions.

Robert MacIver, born in Stornoway in this century, become Lieber Professor of Political Philosophy at Columbia University in America, and was an advisor to the American Government as a result of his reputation as one of America's most eminent social scientists. Thomas Babington MacAulay, the first and only Baron MacAulay of Rothley, the English essayist and historian, was only one generation removed from his Gaelic-speaking ancestors, one of whom was born in the Manse of Harris and

97

himself derived from the MacAulays of Uig. Another MacAulay with the same first names made a fortune in insurance in Canada and funded the setting up of the MacAulay Institute of Soil Research in Aberdeen. Prime Minister of Great Britain, W.E. Gladstone, also had Stornoway connections, with his mother being born in the town. The former Speaker of the House of Commons, a Morrison from North Uist, eventually became Lord Dunrossil. Not so well known, perhaps, is James MacDonald, born in 1771 in Paible, North Uist, who became a minister and was for many years in Germany, where he was a friend of some of the literary giants of his time, including J.G. Herder, Schiller and the more famous Goethe. MacDonald was described as an excellent linguist 'speaking as many languages as there were states in the United States of America'. His main contribution to our knowledge of the Highlands and Islands is a massive Report on Agricultural practices in the Western Isles.

Other 'minor' lights from the islands include the 'Nova Scotia Giant', a MacAskill from Harris, who was the strongest man in that country of his generation, and Donald Morrison, born in Canada of Lewis parents, who became known as the 'Megantic Outlaw', after he killed a man in self-defence and set off one of the longest and most extensive manhunts in Canadian history.

There are today many parts of the world where colonies of island-born natives, or their descendants, can be found, many of whom have, and are still doing so, contributed to the economic and social wellbeing of the countries in which they live. It is more than a passing fancy to consider to what extent the Western Isles might have benefited, had these talents for enterprise, initiative and entrepreneurial adventure been given full rein in their own islands. But perhaps that is the sad fate of the islands: to breed such men and women who are destined to fertilize other communities under different skies.

This enrichment is a continuous process. For instance, in the field of Scottish literature, novelist and poet, Ian Crichton Smith, born in Point, Lewis, has made an outstanding contribution and is still active; as is Derick Thomson, another Lewis native who, though his contribution is more aligned to the Gaelic culture, is widely recognized as being among the best of Scotland's poets. In an earlier decade, Agnes Mure MacKenzie became one of Scotland's most eminent and, needless to say, sympathetic historians.

6. Island communities

It has taken the people of the Western Isles much longer than the folk of Orkney and Shetland to establish firm and stable bases for their economy. The Northern Isles have always had the advantage of lying in the mainstream of the North Atlantic shipping trade between Europe, Scandinavia in particular, and North America. For instance, Stromness in Orkney became an ideal base for whaling ships before they sailed into the Arctic seas for their hunting expeditions, though one could easily conceive Stornoway to be a suitable port for the operations of that industry. Yet only Harris, of all the Western Isles, experienced in the early years of this century a peripheral whaling interest and that was long after the heyday of the industry. Though it must be said that after World War II many islanders took part in the whaling industry based on South Georgia in the South Atlantic.

Again, the agricultural situation which exists in Orkney, and to a lesser extent in the Shetland islands, was more favourable than in the Western Isles where, apart from the machair land, poor soil conditions and the lack of real incentives under the 1886 Crofting Act militated against development and thus progress in land use techniques. Another important factor has been the manner in which the Western Isles, before 1974, were split up for local government purposes into two divisions: under the old Inverness-shire County Council (Harris and the southern isles) and Ross and Cromarty County Council (Lewis only). With the seats of local government located in far away Inverness and Dingwall, distance placed the Western Isles at a serious disadvantage in the provision of public services and related facilities. Orkney and Shetland, on the other hand, have benefited from a long history of indigenous local government, being in relatively full control of their own economic and social development. There is nothing like having one's own people in charge of one's own local affairs!

The fact that Stornoway itself managed to become a significant port for trade shipping from the early years of last century was due to the determination of some of the town's merchants and leading lights. Even so, that prosperity tended to be concentrated in the town and its immediate hinterland. As a burgh it had, of necessity, to look to itself and any benefits which derived from its status could only be passed to Lewis in

Croft house at Lemreway, Lewis

general as minor spin-offs. However, as a commercial centre it drew in a commuting workforce from the island's townships which more than appreciated the opportunity of gaining worthwhile employment earning incomes which supplemented the meagre rewards available from crofting.

That general pattern of the economy of the Western Isles today is that described in professional jargon as 'economic pluralism', which simply means a broad base of income-generating activities, involving anything from large-scale industry (such as Harris Tweed) to craft enterprises, from the provision of services to fish-farming. Self-employment is an integral part of the islands' economy, with, for instance, crofter-weavers being classed as self-employed. The job spectrum is limited in its scope, particularly for young school-leavers, whether or not they are well-qualified. Another aspect of the employment pattern is that there is a tradition of multiple job holding, which has provided some degree of job security. A fisherman might also be a tweed weaver, with both occupations filling in the slumps as they occur. So far as females are concerned, there has always been a low activity rate for women; indeed, female activity rates in the Western Isles are the lowest of all Scottish Regions and Islands Areas.

Most firms in the islands tend to be small; there are very few medium-large employers. The general lack of Local Authority finance has created difficulty in attracting outside industrial interests to come to the Western Isles; relative remoteness tends to militate against the setting up of large low-value operations. However, there is great potential for the production of high-value, light-weight components – for example, for the electronics industry – as the island of Skye has demonstrated in recent years.

One bright light on the scene is the recent establishment of multi-function community co-operatives, whose activities have generated small pockets of employment in many rural areas. Some of these have been eminently successful while others are still struggling to find a formula for success. The co-operative at Ness, one of the first ever to be set up, went into liquidation in 1986 for a number of reasons, not entirely related to the enthusiasm which initiated the co-operative in the first place. Government initiatives such as Job Creation and Community Programmes have produced little long-term employment prospects, though they have contributed to the general improvement of facilities in rural areas, such as peat roads.

The impact of offshore oil has only recently appeared in the Western Isles, with an onshore construction yard at Arnish Point just outside Stornoway, which is exposed to the fluctuations in the oil industry and thus has not been an entirely stable element in the economy. Though there are prospects of oil in the Minch waters and in the Atlantic to the west of the Hebrides, these are long-term possibilities and have made little impact on the more immediate requirements of the overall employment scene.

Public service provides the main employment opportunities in the service sector of the economy, with its share amounting to some 60 per cent. The fact that it provides labour opportunities in remote areas and particularly for part-time employment tends to make it something of an economic sheet-anchor for many people. Tourism provides a valuable, if short, seasonal employment sector, but to date it has not been developed or marketed to any great extent. The cost of taking one's car and family across the Minch on the ferries tends to deter many from visiting the islands. It is a fact of island life that it costs more to fly from Stornoway to Glasgow than it does to fly across the Atlantic to New York from London.

In sum, island communities still find life something of a struggle. The fact that the future is seen as hopeful and full of potential based on their indigenous resources underlines the determination of the islesfolk to work out their own salvation. Self-help has ever been the keynote to long-term survival.

Digging potatoes, Eoropie, Ness, Lewis. The crofter enjoys a greater choice of crop (potatoes, cereals, rye, oats) on the more fertile or machair land

Crofting

In 1886 the crofter was written into the Statute Books of Great Britain as a legal entity, by means of the Crofters Act of that year. The route by which this status was achieved, to give the crofter security of tenure in particular, was long and hard, winding its tortuous way through Highland history: the Clearances, mass emigration, bloody confrontations with the law and military forces, hunger and starvation, crop failures, social and economic depression and, finally, the necessary politicization of the crofting movement to gain a measure of basic human rights.

In simple terms, a crofter is one who is the tenant of a few acres of arable land, with a share in land lying outwith the township crofts, called common grazings. This might sound an ideal situation, but the reality is often a difficult way of life. The croft land itself is rather poor in quality, with its fertility artificially encouraged by, in the past, cartloads of seaweed, and today with the use of chemical fertilizers. Few crofts actually provide an income which could support a family; the vast majority are able only to provide subsistence living. The common grazings are often little better in quality: mostly peatland and very rough grassland used for the grazing of sheep. In fact it is, in the islands, the sheep which constitute a 'cash crop' rather than any produce grown on the croft itself. Indeed, one can see in Lewis today many crofts now lying derelict, covered with rushes where the drainage systems have been neglected, and being encroached by heather and bracken. There are crofts in the vicinity of Stornoway which have been completely grassed over, occasionally for a couple of sheep to graze over, or else used as a green sward or lawn at the back of the croft house.

In more fertile areas, such as those with machair land, the crofts tend to be fairly well used, for potatoes, mainly, but cereals are also grown. Rye is rather more tolerant of salty winds and sandy soil and as it grows it tends to draw up the companion crop, oats, with it towards the light and protects the ears from the wind.

While cattle tends to be a traditional interest in the Uists, in Lewis and Harris it is the ubiquitous sheep which is relied on to produce an income. It has been reckoned that the value of the sheep in Lewis on the hoof is worth over £5 million. The present subsidies for sheep are a great temptation and often more sheep are kept than is good for the land. Sheep crop the grass with their teeth, and nibble very close to the ground, reducing vegetation to a minimum. In addition, their droppings tend to be acidic, which makes the land on which they graze sour and unproductive. Cattle, on the other hand, tear grass with their long tongues and are the better grazing animal for those areas of common grazings which have been reclaimed by the addition of lime and fertilizer to produce new swards of grass. The recently-revived interest in Lewis towards cattle is a portent for the future and is long overdue. In the Uists, the agricultural economy has always been based on the rearing of beef cattle. The cattle are mostly a blend of Highland and Island strains, which gives a breed called 'Luing'; some cattle show the familiar Highland strain more than others, with shaggy, wide-horned heads. The calves are highly valued and mainland buyers come to the Uist sales to buy these animals,

Training unit leaving Balivanich Airport (over)

which are in peak condition after having spent a summer on rich machair grasses and flowers.

The main disincentive to cattle-rearing in the Western Isles is the problem of providing wintering facilities, a capital-intensive item in these days of high costs. The potential for change from sheep to cattle stock is good and may yet be realised, to reflect the times when Hebridean cattle constituted a major element in the economy of the islands. In 1845 the entry for Stornoway in the *New Statistical Account for Scotland* records near that town '. . . there is a square mile of moor enclosed for a cattle tryst where several thousand head are exposed for sale and 2000 at least change hands in two days. From 20 to 30 drovers come from the Mainland and some from England.' When one considers that this was an average annual yield, the cattle stock of Lewis was considerable in those days.

Cattle from Harris and the Uists were usually shipped across the Minch to Skye. The 'Statistical Account' mentions an average of 200 beasts from Harris being exported annually, while the Uist figures were often very much higher than those for Lewis. The lot of these beasts was never a happy one. Cattle had to swim across the narrows between islands – this was the case until recently at Vatersay – and across the fords connecting North and South Uist to Benbecula. They were then packed tightly into boats strongly built for the trade to prevent them from falling overboard. The subsequent journey across the Minch was not always easy sailing for man or beast. In 1808 a wherry was wrecked while bringing cattle across from North Uist. Three of the crew of four were lost, with the survivor keeping himself alive with the blood of some of the surviving cattle until he was rescued. Arriving on Skye, the cattle were driven across that island and then had to swim the waters of the Sound of Sleat from Kylerhea to Bernera on the Glenelg side of the Scottish mainland, before trekking a weary road down to the cattle trysts at Crieff and Falkirk.

At the present time about 77 per cent of the land in the Western Isles is held in crofting tenure, with some 6000 individual crofting units, of which less than 80 per cent of all holdings are capable of providing some 40 standard man-days per annum and less than one per cent are classified as full-time agricultural holdings. A 'man-day' is defined as a full day's work, from which it is obvious that crofting at its best can only be regarded as a part-time activity, with crofters of necessity having to look for other work to reach an acceptable level of income per annum.

A recent boost to improve land use in the islands came with an Integrated Development Programme, funded from UK Government sources and the Common Market. Valued at £20 million, it began in 1982 for a period of five years. The important element of the Programme was 'integration', which has been interpreted as meaning the development of all possible croft-related activities, including land improvement and extending crofting interests into such industries as fish-farming, crafts, weaving, tourism and the like. The Programme came to an end in

Machair conservation in progress at Gowry beach, North Tolsta

1987, and hopes to extend the scheme for a further two years came to nothing. Now it remains for the beneficiaries of the Programme to build on the foundations prepared by the IDP.

One unusual land-owner in Lewis is the Stornoway Trust. In 1918 the ownership of Lewis passed into the hands of Lord Leverhulme, one of the most enterprising, innovative and entrepreneurial industrialists in Britain, whose fortune was based on soap. He immediately embarked on a programme of industrial development, based on Stornoway, and the fish-processing possibilities inherent in the indigenous fishing industry. In brief, many of his schemes came to nothing and in 1923 he decided to leave Lewis for pastures new (Harris), with only one question to be answered:

How was he to dispose of the island? Despite the bitter disappointment he obviously felt keenly his inability to do 'something in a small way for the permanent benefit of its fine people' and decided to give Lewis to its folk.

Any crofter who wanted to become the owner of his few acres was open to accept his croft as a gift from Leverhulme. But few took up the offer, for on acceptance the crofter would immediately lose his security of a fixed rateable value and lose access to grants and other funds only available for crofting activities. On the other hand, the Town Council of Stornoway accepted the gift which consisted of Lews Castle and its woodland policies, the Parish of Stornoway (which extended northwards from Arnish Moor as far as Tolsta, 14 miles away), all the large farms and all the sporting and fishing rights. The whole gift was to be administered by the Stornoway Trust. It is unique in Britain: a body looking after an estate of some 64,000 acres which is wholly in community ownership. Trustees are drawn from the community and are elected by secret ballot by persons who appear in the current Valuation Roll as owning or occupying property on the Estate. This means that while the owner or tenant of a property has a vote, the rest of his family do not. But tenants of Comhairle nan Eilean within Stornoway parish have a vote just as surely as do the crofters on the Estate. The Trust is run by a factor, who is the employee of the Trustees.

Because of lack of funds, the Trust has over the years been unable to be little more than a caretaker of its lands. However, it has helped all kinds of developments in and around Stornoway by making land available for industrial and commercial enterprises and land for new Local Authority housing and private dwellings.

In recent years a new significant influx of funds has enabled the Trust to look to schemes which are directly related to crofting, such as an experimental afforestation belt plantation and a salmon hatchery. The Trust has also helped with Job Creation Projects sponsored by crofting townships, and has given financial encouragement to school educational trips and Gaelic choirs attending the National Mod, which is the annual musical and literary festival of the Gaelic world.

The Stornoway Trust Estate stands out in stark contrast to much of the rest of Lewis, which was parcelled off in Lord Leverhulme's time and sold for a few pence per acre. These were then bought up by individuals, private consortia and institutions. Their presence on the island has been far from beneficial to the crofting interests on these estates, which are mainly used for sporting activities.

Fishing

Fishing is a major contributor to the economy of the Western Isles and is carried out mainly as a full-time occupation or, to a lesser extent, as a part-time activity in conjunction with crofting or weaving. The industry

Salmon farm at Leurbost in Lewis. The farming of fish represents a complementary approach to the role of crofting on land

employs about 6 per cent of the working population, with around 400 full-time fishermen, 86 part-time and well over 100 ancillary workers whose livelihood depends on the industry. The Western Isles fishing fleet comprises some 120 boats between 30 ft and 75 ft in length, involved in catching white fish and shellfish. The former catch is worth £1 million annually, while the latter, because of its higher level of market appeal, runs to over £2 million yearly. Fish processing plants located throughout the islands deal with white fish and nephrop landings, and two reduction plants at Stornoway and Ardvenish on Barra produce fishmeal and oil, largely from pelagic species of fish.

The history of the fishing industry is worth a book on its own. Effectively dating from the seventeenth century, it has seldom been one of direct local involvement. Capital and other resources, including initiatives, have always come from outside the islands, as the local population was never in the happy circumstance of building up the funds needed to purchase boats – until, in the later years of the herring fishing, crewmen working on Scottish boats saved up enough cash to go it alone. But by then, just after World War I, the herring industry went into a slow process of decline and the benefits accruing from local control were never fully realised.

At the present time the once rich waters of the Minch are now sadly depleted of species and local boats can often spend a day at sea and return with little more than a box or two, hardly enough to cover fuel, wages and expenses, including loan payments on the capital needed to buy the boat in the first place. When one considers that a new boat could cost upwards of £500,000, lack of fish can be a serious problem for both owners and crew.

The advent of the steam trawler at the turn of this century was the start of the gradual destruction of the Minch as an important fishing area. Their trawls scoured the sea beds which also destroyed the breeding grounds for some species of white fish. The imposition of the three-mile limit round British shores helped to preserve the integrity of the waters round the islands' shores but persistent illegal trawling, coupled with the lack of adequate protection afforded by too few fishery protection vessels, soon depleted stocks. Today boats can now trawl up to the shoreline, no thanks to Common Market Regulations which foreign boats exploit to their maximum advantage. Broad Bay, just north of Stornoway, is designated a controlled area but is still, on occasion, plundered by vessels whose profit motive provides a greater incentive than does conservation. The days are long past when one could take a small boat a mile or two from the shore, drop a hand line and arrive home an hour later with a good catch of haddock, mackerel and saithe.

Though the species is something of a cash salvation for many local boats, the sand eel is being exploited far in excess of its ability to sustain its numbers. Thousands of tons are taken from the sea each year, thus depriving other species which feed on the eels as an important food resource. Like the herring, now subjected to close season orders, the Minch fishing will eventually disappear, and that sooner rather than later.

What is now urgently required is some form of repressive conservation if the remaining stocks of fish are to have any reasonable chance of providing the Western Isles fishing fleet with some degree of continuity into the future. There was always an historic right for several European countries to fish in UK waters, but this has expanded as a result of Britain's entry into the Common Market. Now, with the Community's catching power being added to that of the British fleet, one sees the inevitable consequence in the current poor catches of the local boats.

The formation some years ago of the Stornoway Fishermen's Co-operative introduced a much-needed cohesive element into the organis-ation of the industry. It has preserved the fishing industry in Stornoway, where it might have died altogether, because it looks after the catching, buying, processing and selling of the product.

The shellfish side of the industry has now assumed great importance. As a young lad the writer remembers going down to the harbour for a pail filled to the brim with prawns given away free by the fishermen, because they were a nuisance catch among the more prized white fish. It is a different story today! In the Uists the emphasis is on lobsters and crab; the former, after being caught, are kept alive in lobster ponds and tanks at Grimsay Island. The fishing has been given a major boost with the erection of a processing factory, opened in 1986, at Gramsdale on Benbecula. Since the crab fishery in Uist waters began to take off in the late 1970s there was always a pressing need for a local processing facility. This has now been provided with funds from the Highlands and Islands Development Board and the Integrated Development Programme. The new factory will bring much-needed employment to the area and present an opportunity for shell-fishermen to diversify from lobster, since prawn fishing, salmon production and mussel cultivation are all on the increase in Uist. The factory is capable of processing all of these species.

Perhaps the most dramatic development on the fishing scene in the Western Isles is the commercial growing of salmon. A Report in 1975 identified 3000 hectares of potentially farmable seawater in the UK, of which 1300 hectares, or 40 per cent, is in the Western Isles, which has the additional asset of being unpolluted, disease-free waters. Salmon-farming has now taken off in a big way in Lewis, Harris and South Uist and has been successful in making inroads into a market for farmed salmon, which has been until recently wholly commandeered by the Norwegians. Demand still exceeds supply and will continue to do so for some years to come, by which time, no doubt, local processing units will be established on the islands to provide still more employment opportunities, particularly for young folk who are being trained for the industry at the Technical College in Inverness.

Another sea-related industry is the collecting and drying of seaweed. The alginate industry has had a long historical association in the Western Isles, from the days at the turn of the nineteenth century when the burning of kelp seaweed produced the ash necessary for making glass. At its peak, in the early 1970s, the harvesting drying of seaweed (chiefly the species *ascophyllum nodosum*) gave employment to about 50 part-time cutters and about the same number employed in drying plants in Lewis and North and South Uist. Today, only the plants at Lochmaddy and Keose, in Lewis, still operate. In 1980 the Keose plant was closed down, but opened a year later when the factory was taken over by a workers' co-operative, which is now financially viable and turning to other means to diversify the operation.

The main problem facing the Western Isles fishing fleet is its age, with many of the boats now approaching their twentieth year in hard working conditions. Despite the hope generated by the full implications of the Integrated Development Programme, fishing vessels were specifically excluded from its financial benefits. The result has been, in some cases, that fishermen have abandoned their bigger boats for smaller vessels to concentrate on shell-fishing. But until a solution is found to bridge the financial gap between the present value of fishing boats and the cost of replacement with new boats, the future facing the fleet is bleak.

Harris Tweed

The weaving of woollen cloth has been a domestic activity throughout the Highlands and Islands for many centuries. Rents were often paid in blankets or plaiding, though the cloth was mainly produced for the immediate household. In the early years of last century, the estate of Harris came into the ownership of the Earls of Dunmore, the first non-native proprietors. The weaving skills of two sisters, from Strond in South Harris, came to the notice of the Countess of Dunmore. Known as the 'Paisley Sisters', they had both received training of weaving at Paisley and were thus able to produce cloth of a higher quality than that of their neighbours, which the Countess was quick to realise had a significant market potential. However, production of the cloth had to be sufficient to meet the demand, and she sent some young Harris girls to the Scottish mainland for training in the weaving of intricate patterns. In this small way the Harris Tweed industry was started. Initially the customers were in the top income bracket, always on the lookout for a cloth which could withstand much wear in outdoor activities as they hunted, fished and shot on their estates. But it was not long before other customers were eager to have garments made of the hard-wearing tweed.

The popularity of the cloth grew to such proportions that demand often outstripped supply, and other islands began to take an active part. About 1877 South Uist tweeds found their way to the London market. Lewis, however, was conspicuous by its absence for some years until, slowly, Lewis weavers turned to the loom, though their cloth was called Harris Tweed to take advantage of the cachet which the Harris cloth had so successfully exploited.

There were problems, however. All the processes involved in making the cloth were hand-done, from washing and dyeing the wool to carding, spinning, warping, weaving and then finishing. By the turn of the century it was obvious that, to keep up with the demand, some of the processes had to be carried out by machines. The first process to receive attention was carding. This was a slow task and extremely tiring. In 1900 a carding mill

1 *Carloway, Lewis. Contrasting cultivated or machair land and rugged hills, a perspective typical of Western Isles geography.*

2 Opposite *A Harris Tweed weaver, Shawbost, Lewis.*

3 Above *Variety Stores mobile shop visits Northbay, Barra.*

4 Opposite *A man's best friend . . . is his tractor. A Crofter in Mariveg, Lewis.*

5 Above *Shearing time near Brevig in Barra.*

6 *Highland games and dances are not just traditions kept alive for the tourists. The Borve Games, Barra Festival.*

7 *Borve, Harris.*

8 *A single standing stone at Langas and a prospect towards Locheport in North Uist.*

was erected at Tarbert, Harris, with machinery powered by water. Three years later another carding mill was built in Stornoway and both facilities not only eliminated a bottleneck in production but actually increased demand. This was catered for by introducing spinning mills in the island. Later, other processes were added to ensure the consistent quality of the product. While all this was going on, the cloth was, as it is today, still woven by crofters in their own homes.

Over the decades it is Stornoway which has emerged as the centre of the Harris Tweed industry with the bulk of the cloth being woven by Lewis crofters. A small amount of the cloth is still woven in Harris and elsewhere by more traditional methods. A mill at Shawbost on the west side of Lewis, which started operations in 1915 in a very small way, now employs about 40 people and is the largest industrial operation of its kind in the whole of the Western Isles, outside Stornoway.

The weavers are classed as self-employed and are thus dependent on the aggressive selling techniques of the mills and the Harris Tweed Association, which have won markets for Harris Tweed all over the world. Inevitably, as fashions change, so does the demand for the cloth fluctuate. Even allowing for this, the industry has played a vital role in the economy of Lewis in particular. There are about 750 weavers at present, with the spinning and finishing mills employing some 350 people. Over 80 per cent of the cloth is exported, an achievement which has earned the industry recognition – with the Queen's Award to Industry coming to Lewis a number of times in recent years.

The important point must be made that, though the initial and finishing processes are carried out by the mills, every single web of cloth is woven by crofter-weavers in their own homes. Were it not so, the cloth and its Orb trade mark would not be protected by law and many imitations would appear on the market, thus placing at risk a vital island industry. Recent attempts to recruit young blood into the industry have been successful, in the form of training courses at Lews Castle College, thus ensuring that, as older weavers leave the occupation, the number of weavers required to cater for demand is maintained at an optimum level. New weavers are helped by the Harris Tweed Loom fund in purchasing new looms and bobbin-winding machines, which together can cost anything up to £7000.

Also in the area of textiles comes knitting which, like tweed, has been a home industry for centuries. Almost in parallel to the development of the tweed industry in Harris, knitting assumed a significant economic importance. In 1859 an agency was opened in Edinburgh for the sale of both tweeds and knitted goods, the latter the produce of many Harris women, whose skills with the needles ensured articles of a quality which the market was only too eager to snap up. In the 1870s, in Harris alone, some 400 people were engaged in knitting, earning valuable cash to supplement an otherwise subsistence economy. Stockings and gansies were the main items, the latter displaying both imagination and innovation in their patterns.

Only in recent years has knitting begun to achieve something of its former popularity, though the market has firmly expressed a greater interest in hand-knitted garments than in those produced by machines. In fact, the once-thriving machine-knitting industry has gone into decline. A few years ago some six knitwear factories were being hailed as a new enterprise with a future. They have now all but closed down, with only a few small companies producing knitwear – the largest being in Daliburgh, followed by others in Stornoway.

The demand for hand-knits remains high, however, with garments sold to the market mainly through the agencies of the community co-operatives.

Many of the designs of gansies are traditional, though many have been lost over the years. The island of Eriskay has, however, done much to revive patterns associated with the Hebrides. Unlike the usual vertical configurations, the hebridean gansey is patterned in blocks set horizontally, each containing a different symbol. The patterns include representations of starfish, anchors, marriage lines and diamonds, the latter traditionally representing the fishing-net.

The crofting township

Crofting has been described as a way of life. Certainly, it takes a certain kind of person to consider taking up a lifetime of struggle with poor land, knowing that the croft itself can never yield an income in proportion to the work needed to keep the land in a sweet and reasonably productive condition. Yet, to become a crofter is the aim of many young folk who look behind the occupation to achieve a high level of personal satisfaction. As a way of life, crofting has much to recommend it. In the first instance, it provides for a unique social structure in its various townships, which often require the creation of communal and self-help bases on which to survive. It has also had a significant impact on the maintenance of linguistic (Gaelic) and cultural values that might otherwise be dispersed and disappear altogether. Crofting provides a keen edge to life, which offers some route to a kind of spiritual satisfaction in which personal ideals can be achieved.

The visitor can often sense the world of difference between the picturesque villages of the English countryside and the townships of the Highlands and Islands, which are equally picturesque though not perhaps so photogenic. English settlements have, in the main, a long stable history of close communal association, together with a history of tightly-controlled regulation imposed by the local feudal manor and its lord. The surrounding countryside is witness to centuries of careful cultivation by the toiling villein and serf, and the total encompassing atmosphere is one of slow-moving, almost Utopian contentment: at least that is the impression the visitor receives.

On the other hand, many crofting townships, while some are indeed of long standing, have a much shorter history, having been created by the harsh displacement of populations in the last century or so. Many of the present-day townships are products of the crofters' immediate forebears: men and women who often had to make the very soil from an alchemic mixture of seaweed and crushed stones, having been forced to settle on the most infertile and rocky land possible. A tour southwards on the eastern coast of Harris, from Tarbert to Rodel, is visual history at first hand: settlements built up from nothing, with the moorland greenings the product of long hard work over many decades.

Crofting townships also have an atmosphere of perpetual change, as dwellings, for instance, are revamped from the old vernacular style to ultra-modern design. There are seldom particular features in the township that demonstrate a development from feudal bond to freehold: no village square, no village pub to act as a neutral area for discussion of local problems, no visible memorials to the war dead and none of the outward trappings that conventionally indicate a close-knit community. Yet, the crofting township *is* a tight social unit, simply because it is the people who are the dynamic elements. The physical environment is merely a stage setting. What the visitor will sense and detect, armed with even a superficial knowledge of the history that brought these townships into being, is a sturdy, healthy attitude and commitment to island life, despite the drawbacks.

There are about 250 crofting townships in the Western Isles. In some cases a single township may be isolated from other townships and forms a settlement on its own; in other cases, several townships may coalesce to form a fairly large settlement. The relationship between the number of crofts in any one township, the size and shape of these crofts, and the proximity and nature of the adjoining townships all contribute to the distinctive form and size of crofting settlements. In general, crofting settlements are located around arable coastal land, particularly the machair land on the western seaboard. Most crofts take the form of linear strips running across contours. Croft houses, and thus settlements, are usually built along roads and the depth of development seldom exceeds two houses. The size of settlement varies quite considerably, depending on factors such as the number of crofts, shape and size of crofts, age of settlement and the proximity of townships. In addition, the place of any individual settlement in the overall pattern or hierarchy of settlements is of importance.

Not all of the houses in a crofting settlement are croft houses. As the number of crofts is, by and large, fixed, and as there is usually a limit of one croft house per croft, any additional dwellings required in a township will take the form of private houses on feus, or Local Authority houses. In

Crofter house enlargement at Doune in Lewis. Crofter houses are working buildings, and the crofters are less concerned than some villagers on the mainland with the architectural 'purity' of the structures

many instances, these latter houses are located on the edge of a crofting township, usually on common grazings, thereby extending what is often already a linear settlement form. Often part of a croft is 'de-crofted', to provide a feu for a private house, say for the ageing parents of a family who wish the son to assume the tenancy of the croft itself.

The importance of the crofting system in influencing settlement development cannot be underestimated. The tenancy of a good croft is often much sought after, particularly by young people. But the system of croft assignation means that young persons may have to wait a considerable length of time before they have an opportunity to obtain a croft, and this may discourage them from remaining in an area. On the other hand, the possession of a croft, with all its attendant financial benefits in grants and subsidies, tends to tie people to that particular area. In order to ensure a holding population, the Local Authority has, over the last decade, followed an active policy of locating both general needs and sheltered housing in the rural areas throughout the Western Isles. The provision of sheltered housing in the crofting townships not only provides the elderly with improved living conditions but also encourages older persons to renounce their crofts in favour of younger persons, thus allowing them to remain in their home area. The provision of general needs housing in the township offers not only a greater choice of housing, but enables young families, without access to a croft, to remain in the area. Then, when a vacant croft appears, they at least have a residential claim for its assignation to them.

Another interesting provision in some townships is the Tigh Ceilidh. In past times one or more houses were identified within the community as the place to go to of an evening in winter, where one not only heard the local gossip and news but storytellers, singers and local bards. In Gaelic a 'ceilidh' means a friendly visit to a neighbour's house and this is what is implied in these new taighean ceilidh: a building used as a community centre where meetings, formal and informal, can be held by youth groups, committees, church services, keep-fit classes, sales of work and the like. These taighean ceilidh provide an important social service and go a long way to recovering the strong community bonds which held a township together in past times.

Community co-operatives

The essential idea behind a community co-operative is to provide a base for an economic activity which requires a pooling of local skill, enterprise, innovation and entrepreneurial ability, all of which help a community not only to identify what it does already, but to establish what it can do. The idea is not new, however. Social and economic co-operation has always been a traditional feature of life in the Western Isles. At an informal level, many crofting and domestic activities are carried out on a community basis or family effort. On another level, the pooling of resources and expertise, such as is the case with the Stornoway Fishermen's Co-operative, makes for a more efficient use of these aspects, leading to a reduction in managerial and other overheads and increased profitability.

Community co-operatives were first established in the Highlands and Islands in 1978, through the agency of the Highlands and Islands Development Board. Each locality which identified a need for its own co-operative had to raise a certain sum of money locally, say £10,000, which was then matched by the HIDB. The co-operatives now number around 23 and are scattered from Orkney and Shetland, through the west coast of the Scottish mainland and as far south as the Isle of Bute. There are seven co-operatives in the Western Isles: Park in Lewis, Scalpay, Harris, Iochdar in South Uist, Eriskay, Barra and Vatersay. The co-operative at

Staff of the Ness Community Co-op – now, sadly, folded

Ness, the first to be set up in 1978, went into voluntary liquidation in 1986.

The co-operatives (called in the Western Isles 'Co-Chomuinn') are basically multi-function businesses run for local benefit and directly owned and controlled by the community in which they operate. Although they are still going through a period of experimentation, they are a

George Wyllie's 'Americana' on exhibition at An Lanntair art gallery, Stornoway

particularly appropriate form of development for areas in which services to the community have declined. The activities of the Western Isles Co-Chumuinn include horticulture, the hire of agricultural machinery, fish farming, building contracting, knitwear production and general retailing. In addition, they have provided both full-time and part-time jobs for local people and thus make a significant contribution to the general economy of their areas.

One of the most successful co-operatives to date has been Co-chommun na Hearadh, the Harris enterprise. Sales revenue in 1984 reached just over £300,000. The headquarters are located in An Clachan, Leverburgh, a specially built building which incorporates the Harris Craft Guild, a tea room, craft shop and a grocery retailing outlet. The co-operative makes regular appearances at Trade Fairs, returning to Harris with healthy order books. For the first time in a number of years, 1986 saw the need to advertise for good quality knitwear to fulfil orders taken at these Fairs, an indication that the general public are willing to support hand-crafted articles with a Hebridean cachet.

Communications

While the strength of any island community lies in its ability to survive on its own resources, situations eventually arise when it is necessary to establish links with the mainland. The Western Isles have not escaped this fact and have contributed to the development of inter- and intra-island communications by sea, initially, and latterly by air.

Sea communications came slowly to the Hebrides, though informal trading links were already established before 1800. In the main, it was Stornoway which benefited from its reputation as a safe harbour and a commercial centre, importing the essentials and the occasional luxury for island living and exporting dried and salted fish, hides, wool, cloth and cattle. In the early years of last century passenger ships plied up and down the west coast of Scotland as far as the River Clyde, and it was not long before the Western Isles beckoned the intrepid traveller to experience the remote and hardly visited islands.

It was not until Sir James Matheson bought Lewis in 1844 that attempts were made to regularize sea communications. At the time, mails and other goods were carried across the Minch to Poolewe, on the Wester Ross coast, usually three times a week. This frequency was thought by Sir James to be a deterrent to Stornoway's development and he arranged for the *Mary Jane* to carry mails on a more frequent and regular basis. Eventually he obtained a subsidy from the Post Office for the service: £1300 to be set against a sum more than ten times that figure, which he bore himself in the provision of the service.

*Lochboisdale, South Uist (*preceding pages*)*

While Sir James Matheson was busy establishing sea connections across the Minch, others were looking for profits from a south-north route carrying goods and passengers. The giant who emerged from the myriad of steamship companies based on the Clyde was David MacBrayne, who, in his late sixties, started a new company with his own name and launched a building programme which gave birth to a long line of ships that were to serve the Western Isles for well over a century. His name is still remembered by the shipping company which now commands much of the ferry trade on Scotland's west coast: Caledonian-MacBrayne Ltd.

Both MacBrayne's ships and those of another, now defunct, company, MacCallum-Orme, plied the Minch waters regularly, connecting Lochmaddy, Lochboisdale, Stornoway and Castlebay with various ports on the mainland: principally, but not exclusively, Oban and Kyle of Lochalsh in Wester Ross. The names of many of these ships are burnt into the memory of an older generation of islesfolk for the way in which their crews maintained a regular service, often in the foulest of weather. The fact that they also called in at many smaller places in the islands, often difficult of access by sea, provided remote townships with a link with the outside world, to say nothing of the essential goods and provisions they brought with them. These communities included Leverburgh and Finsbay, in Harris, Loch Skipport and Loch Eport in the Uists and Northbay on Barra. At one time, just before World War II, the map of the Minch was criss-crossed with the routes taken by the ships of the Hebrides; today the few routes marked on maps give no indication at all of the highly efficient and regular service which the Western Isles once enjoyed.

Another now defunct shipping company was Coast Lines Ltd, which concentrated on a goods only service, though a very limited passenger service was provided. The ships of this Company also called in at remote settlements with livestock, foodstuffs, furniture and other goods. If all this frequent traffic might be surprising today, one has to realise that it was one of the survival elements on which the continuity of many communities depended. It could be said that, were it not for many of these ships, large and small, these same communities might well be deserted by now. Inevitably the economics of providing these services presented some bad headaches for the operators; but it says much for the social conscience of the companies concerned, unlike today, that they continued despite mishaps such as the occasional loss of their vessels. Perhaps the secret was simply that the shipping operators were run by men who maintained a close personal contact with the service they provided for Hebridean communities. In fact, many of the crews were islanders themselves, a factor which went no little way in ensuring that, whatever the weather conditions, the ships got through.

At present, the main ferry services for the Western Isles are run by Caledonian-MacBrayne Ltd. Oban connects with Castlebay and Lochboisdale. Uig, on Skye, connects with Tarbert and Lochmaddy. Stornoway is linked with Ullapool. The car ferries plying the Minch to the Western Isles are the *Claymore*, the *Hebridean Isles* and the *Suilven*.

Inter-island ferries are mainly operated under the agency of the Local Authority, with Scalpay being serviced by Caledonian-MacBrayne. The ferry links are between Leverburgh and Newton Ferry on North Uist, which also serves the island of Berneray. Eriskay is served from Ludac on South Uist and Vatersay is served from Castlebay. A ferry run is also operated between Ludac and Eoligarry at the north end of Barra.

While the larger shipping companies took the lion's share of the Hebridean trade, another class of ships were also doing sterling service, particularly to those communities with no pier facilities. These ships were the 'puffers'. There can scarcely be a person of the older generation on the west coast of Scotland who has not heard of Para Handy, the intrepid skipper of the little coastal trading vessel called the *Vital Spark*, immortalised in the writings of Neil Munro and celebrated both on television and on the big screen in the film *The Maggie*. The latter was typical of a special class of ship which plied the waters off the west coast of Scotland, carrying goods, freight, cargo and coals to those remote communities which had only the sea as their front door to all the necessities of life, to say nothing of a few of life's little luxuries. The approach of the puffer was always heralded by the laboured beat of an engine throbbing in the air, long before a small, squat, almost flush-decked craft came into view. These ships were often the salvation of many coastal and island communities with only a rough track going inland over desolate moor to the nearest town or village. Often, there was no pier or landing stage, and it was a common sight to see a puffer deliberately stranded on a sandbank or beach, with the crew feverishly discharging cargo before the next full tide refloated her, to chuff her way to another, equally remote, community.

The puffers were hardy craft, able to cope with sudden squalls, tide races, treacherous shoals, narrows, currents, submerged rocks and reefs. The puffer was a functional craft, about 65 ft long with a 17 ft beam; the depth was around 8 ft, which allowed the vessel to make use of the Crinan Canal on the way north from the River Clyde. Most of the puffers could take on around one hundred tons of cargo, which was shifted by a single derrick, mounted on a mast well forward in the bows. The engine was placed aft and covered by a box-like structure. Built for sturdiness with a speed of around seven knots, these craft could well handle the moody seas of the Hebrides and ploughed through the waves to make port often when other vessels had to hove to, to weather foul seas. One puffer, the *Warlight*, built in 1919, braved the Minch waters for over 40 years as she plied between the Butt of Lewis and the Mull of Kintyre. Another was the *Boer*, which was renamed *The Maggie* to star in the film of that name, and so shot to fame overnight, to throw well-earned limelight on the puffers as a species of ship which had, for decades, been quietly performing a valuable service for remote mainland and island communities. Cargoes included coal, timber, bricks, cement, salt, sand, farm equipment, animal feeding-stuffs, potatoes, road-metal chips, sheep, cereals, fencing materials and household furniture. Though these craft have now largely disappeared, a few still survive. They were the base of the fleet started by Messrs Cunningham of Scalpay Island in Harris, more than 50 years ago.

Once a familiar sight on the horizon, only the older folk of the islands will remember them, puffing their way past a headland and tacking a course past hidden reefs as they chugged into primitive landing places. Perhaps somewhere Para Handy's ghostly engineer MacPhail is still too engrossed in his 'penny dreadful' to heed the engine signal from Para Handy, 'himself on the bridge', so that the ship 'coudna dash doon a waterfall', while the rest of the ghostly crew are dozing the slow hours away, dreaming of the return journey to the Clyde and more 'tred' to serve the Hebridean islands. One would like to think so.

It is some 60 years since the first aircraft landed in Stornoway Harbour and the crew treated to a luncheon by the town's civic heads. That landing, and some others, started off some local ideas of having the Western Isles served by a regular air link. In 1934 the first commercial flight from Inverness to Stornoway was launched, though the service was intermittent. The following year saw a regular link between Renfrew, near Glasgow, and Stornoway. The man who got the service literally off the ground was a Captain Roberts, who was the first man to operate an air mail service on behalf of the Canadian Government along the route of the MacKenzie, thus establishing an interesting coincidental link as it was Stornoway's son, Sir Alexander MacKenzie, who discovered the river in the eighteenth century.

From then the frequency of air communications were increased and strengthened, so that today one can fly with British Airways from Stornoway to Inverness and Glasgow and from Benbecula to Glasgow. The inter-island air services are provided by the independent company of Loganair which links Stornoway, Benbecula and Barra, and provides a connection between Glasgow and Barra.

The motor car is a ubiquitous part of the island scene. It was not always so. When Sir James Matheson took over Lewis in 1844 there was only one horse-drawn vehicle on the whole island. Thirty years later 87 wheeled vehicles were using the new roads built with funds made available by Matheson. But for many years afterwards the state of the roads throughout the islands was deplorable: lightly-metalled surfaces which deteriorated rapidly, particularly as the motor car became a standard means of transport for the commuting working population. Only in the last decade or so have main island roads been improved, though much remains to be done. The islands are, at present, served by nearly 700 miles of highway, with an additional 100 miles of unadopted roads, mainly tracks, leading to individual croft houses or small and remote settlements.

The post bus traverses the eastern side of Barra

Many of the roads are still single-track and provided with passing places
with sub-standard horizontal and vertical alignment. They are often
poorly founded on underlying peat, a fact which is often seen in the large
cracks in the tarmacadam surfaces. The roads from Stornoway to Tarbert
and from Lochmaddy to Lochboisdale have been designated the inter-
island route, which also links North Uist, Benbecula and South Uist by
means of causeways. Some townships are still without proper road access,
the prime example being Rhenigidale, located in the wilds north of
Tarbert, although some part of the original seven-mile stony track has
been improved recently, in the face of the usual question: why should
money be spent to provide a road link to a settlement of a couple of dozen
people?

There is no economic answer to such a question, which could easily be
asked of other remote crofting townships. It is, however, the policy of the
Local Authority to provide such services to these communities as would

represent the basic minimum required as an encouragement at least for the folk in these townships to feel that they are part of a much greater whole. Otherwise, voluntary migration would be part of the island scene today. That it is not says much for the long-standing forbearance of the islanders who, having been neglected for decades by other Local Authorities, are now beginning to feel they are contributing in some small way to the maintenance of the island population. The lack of opportunities for crofters to take up second jobs is limited, thus depressing the average annual income per household. In general the level of income in the Western Isles is well below the national average, reflecting the differences between national and local economies and the dependence on manual and low technology employment in the islands.

Education

The attitude of islanders to education has always been two-headed. The much-quoted phrase used well over a century ago was that education 'gave our children wings to fly away', in the sense that once young people became aware that their academic achievements were of little use in the islands they went farther afield to seek careers and to achieve their personal goals. On the other hand, it has always been recognized that a broad education opens avenues to the formation of a cultured attitude to life.

One of the main problems in providing education in a bilingual community is that the education system in national terms does not wholly cater for regional variations derived from culture, language and history. Education, as it is provided at present by the State, tends to influence the attitudes and opinions of children from their earliest years and induces in them an outlook which distances them from their native backgrounds. Indeed, the predominance of an English education – and this is not meant in a purely linguistic sense – has created in island children a sense of dislocation from their community history. Many island children find themselves entering university and then, after graduation, discover that their new-won social status and qualifications are incompatible with working in their home communities.

In one ten-year period it was estimated that 1200 young people had left the island of Lewis alone to qualify in higher education, and were, largely, unable to return to give their native island the benefit of their degrees. This export of brains is one of the reasons for the lack of vitality in many Highland and Island communities and, indeed, the reason why some communities have fought the decisions of their Local Authorities tooth and nail, in order to retain enough of an educational provision in their locality to ensure that facilities are available – so that their children can be educated for the needs of the community rather than for industry and commerce in Scotland and England.

Secondary school pupils en route to the Nicolson Institute are bused from Gravir to Stornoway

Because of the scattered nature of the island communities, the provision of education in the Western Isles is expensive, a fact which places great pressure on the Local Authority's finances. The only six-year secondary school in the islands is the Nicolson Institute at Stornoway, to which academically inclined pupils from the Lewis hinterland, Harris and the southern isles must go to prepare for entry to University or other higher education institutions. Of necessity, these children are boarded out in homes in the town or else accommodated in hostels. This enforced break from a previous familiar home-based background has had serious effects on some children. The costs involved in daily, weekly and end-of-term trips home is another financial burden on the Authority, absorbing valuable cash resources which could otherwise be applied to upgrading the many school buildings which are in need of improvement and renovation. The necessary duplication of teaching and equipment resources for the many scattered primary schools involves more expense.

Attempts by the Local Authority to centralize these resources have been attacked by parents threatened with primary school closures. The school is often more than a functional building, and is often seen as a symbol of stability within a community. The building acts as a focal point for meetings and other activities. Once it closes the community loses heart and withers away.

A move to offer the southern isles an educational facility to cater for up to sixth-year pupils has been started at Linaclate, Benbecula, which will remove an educational and social disadvantage from which the southern isles have suffered for many years. It will mean, once the school is opened in 1988, that over one hundred pupils can complete their education at a reasonable distance from their homes instead of having, as at present, to travel all the way to Stornoway. While the provision of basic education is important, the extension into further education is just as essential to allow youngsters who prefer to enter commercial and industrial occupations to take up these options.

The history of vocational education in the islands is full of interest and has been an important factor in the social and economic wellbeing of the islands. As far back as 1711, the minister newly appointed to St Kilda wrote: '... nothing had been taught for many a dark and dreary generation but the art of catching fish and solan geese, for the wretched support of mere animal life'. While his attitude may be forgiven, he failed to recognize that even in such a remote community, instruction in subjects and activities essential for the continuity of the island settlement was an important element for its survival into the future.

It is much the same today, where many communities are dependent on the skills acquired by young people in various trades and occupations essential for their economic stability: for every lawyer there is a need for ten engineers to repair boats and agricultural machinery.

In the past much of the education provisions, apart from the three Rs, were geared to the teaching of hand skills. In 1762 a plan was proposed for the introducing, growing and spinning of flax into Lewis, including the setting up of a 'spinning school in Stornoway'. The scheme got off the ground in the following year and nearly 150 names appeared on the school's roll, more than twice the number in a similar school in the much larger town of Inverness. By the end of 1765 more than 400 girls, equipped with a reel and spinning wheel, had passed successfully through the school. Indeed the production of skilled spinning expertise in such numbers actually created a glut on the market, to the extent that Lewis yarn had to be sent to Belfast and Glasgow for weaving into cloth. By 1800 there were no fewer than eight spinning schools all maintained by the MacKenzie-Seaforths, who owned Lewis. The main feature of this kind of educational provision was that, while the island folk were in general reluctant to put their children forward for elementary education, they were not hesitant in enrolling them for instruction in those skills and arts from which some economic gain was possible. The medium of instruction

The school teacher arrives on Vatersay for the day's classes

was Gaelic, which may account for the fact that Gaelic now contains a large number of words relating to the spinning, warping and weaving of cloth of various types, with an equally large number of words relating to parts of looms, wheels and the like. These schools continued with great success until the nationwide substitution of cheaper cotton from the United States sounded their death knell.

Schools of industry then took their place. In Stornoway in 1848 a Female Industrial School was built which can still be seen on Keith Street. Started by Lady Matheson, wife of Sir James, who bought Lewis in 1844, the school offered instruction in the domestic arts, needlework, sewing and knitting, with other academic subjects included in the curriculum. It lasted until the beginning of this century, when some 'technical' subjects were offered by the Nicolson Institute, the main education institution in the town.

Technical education, *per se*, only appeared in the Western Isles in 1951, with the then defunct Lews Castle being converted into a Technical College. The subjects offered included building construction and navigation and seamanship. The latter enabled many young men from the Western Isles to make their careers in the British Merchant Service from Able Seamen to Captains. Textiles was also on offer for those interested in working in the Harris Tweed industry. Today, the technical education provision is now accommodated in new buildings where anything from carpentry to computing is available for all young persons in the Western Isles. Many of the courses are carefully designed so that successful students can find gainful employment in the islands. Recently a crofting-weaver course for young school-leavers has proved something of a success and is a portent for the future in that young people can take up crofting, and all its related activities such as fish-farming, and be reasonably assured of an active and purposeful career for life. At long last it can be said that education now feeds its products back into the community.

One interesting feature of education in the Western Isles is its commitment to the Local Authority's policy of bilingualism. Gaelic is introduced into the primary curriculum at appropriate points as a formal part of the teaching process and then carried over into the secondary sector on a voluntary basis. The aim of the formal education provision is to enable children from a Gaelic-speaking background to become literate and competent in the use of both English and Gaelic to a level comparable with that achieved in English by their peers elsewhere; and to provide adequate facilities throughout school for children from a non-Gaelic-speaking background to learn Gaelic as a second language, thus enabling them to integrate better into communities which are largely Gaelic in language, culture and character. In general terms, the bilingual pro-gramme has been successful and it only remains for other agencies to offer opportunities for the use of Gaelic in the normal day-to-day working life. These opportunities do, in fact, exist. One can write to the Local Authority using Gaelic and get a reply in Gaelic. In such ways is the future of Gaelic assured, at least in the Western Isles.

Local Government

Before 1974, all Local Government in Scotland was administered through a system of County Councils, City Councils and Burgh Councils. In the Western Isles, Lewis was attached to Ross and Cromarty on the Scottish mainland, the result of a long and historical association going back to 1661, when the boundaries of the Earldom of Ross were changed and Lewis went with Ross as part of the possessions of the Lordship of the Isles. Harris and the rest of the southern isles were part of Inverness-shire County Council, which was, in terms of geographical spread, the biggest local authority in the British Isles. Each island had its own Parishes which elected councillors to represent them on the County Council. Stornoway, being the only Burgh in the Western Isles, had its own Burgh Council and had a rateable value which exceeded that of the County 'town', Dingwall.

Because of this financial 'clout', added to that of the Lewis parish councillors, representing Uig, Barvas, and Lochs, Lewis tended to get a significant share of the money available for public services. Harris and the southern isles had no such political advantage and, as a result, suffered many decades of neglect, evidenced in poor housing conditions, inadequate roads, few water and drainage schemes, no street lighting and so on.

Then, when the Government of the day decided to change the structure of local government in Britain, a new picture emerged. So far as the Western Isles was concerned, all the islands came under a new local authority: the Western Isles Islands Council, or Comhairle nan Eilean. It is a 'most-purpose' authority in that, while it has full control over most decisions, it shares with Highland Regional Council such services as Police, Fire and Rateable Assessors, to the costs of which Orkney Islands Council and Shetland Islands Council also contribute.

The creation of Comhairle nan Eilean to look after the interests of the Western Isles was seen as a chance for the islanders to prove that they had the determination and ability to succeed in a context where previous local authorities had failed. Huge problems, however, had to be faced, not least the small sum of money that could be raised from the rates. For instance, virtually all crofting holdings, including the houses, attract a 50 per cent 'crofting derating' because they are classed as agricultural holdings, and amount to 57 per cent of the total Western Isles housing stock. Thus a house in Stornoway paying £500 per annum in rates is twice the sum payable on an exactly similar property in a crofting township. Because of this situation, Comhairle nan Eilean is heavily dependent on Government funding in Rates Support Grants. This, in fact, makes a mockery of the so-called independence of the islands, which are still controlled and limited effectively in what can be spent on much-needed public services – including the building of local authority housing to cater for the long waiting list, currently running at over 600.

Another problem facing the new authority was the legacy of neglect of the former County Councils' provisions in the islands. Even today some 20 per cent of housing stock in the Western Isles is below 'tolerable standard'. Thus, Comhairle nan Eilean has had an uphill task in providing minimum services and facilities, starting almost from a bed-rock base. That many crofting townships now have proper water and drainage schemes, public lighting, housing and decent roads is a credit to the authority, having achieved these within the constraints of its limited budgets in the ten years since its inception.

The authority's biggest expenditure is on education, which accounts for more than 40 per cent of the total income from rates, support grants

School-leavers can find it easier to defeat an electronic opponent than to find secure employment in the islands

As a 'most-purpose' authority, the Comhairle nan Eilean shares with the
Highland Regional Council services such as the Police – seen here with protestors
at an anti-cruise missile sit-down

and other revenues. This arises from the scattered nature of the
settlements in the Western Isles and the fact that many schools are old and
in need of refurbishment, if not replacement in some cases. The
Government's policy on tenants being enabled to purchase their local
authority house has placed an intolerable burden on Comhairle nan
Eilean. For every house taken out of Local Authority housing stock in this
way at, say, £12,000, it costs over £40,000 to put its replacement into the
stock. With a waiting list of over 600 people waiting for a council house
one can hardly imagine the astronomical sum involved in catering for
those who are officially homeless. And it is not just the sum needed to
build a new house which has to be considered; there are borrowing
charges to be paid – all out of the annual income available to the authority.

The authority is also faced with restrictions placed on it by
Government control in the full exercise of its statutory duties. This is seen
in the agonizing decisions which have to be taken in the allocation of

finance and resources for social services, catering for both young and old. At the present time, to obtain an equitable distribution of the money available over the whole range of social services, charges have to be made for home helps who attend to old people in their own homes. At one time this service was free. Another indication of how hard-pressed the authority is for cash was the recent cancellation of all evening classes for both recreational and vocational subjects. When a penny increase on the rates in the Western Isles raises less than £40,000, the authority's councillors and officials often feel that they live more on a bed of thistles than roses.

In recent years a black and ominous cloud has been gathering on the horizon of the future. Year by year an increasing proportion of its total cash resources is being absorbed in the funding of debt. The current proportion is running at nearly 25 per cent, a high figure when one considers the authority is far from wealthy, is still trying to correct the deplorable legacies left it by the County Councils before 1974, and having to work under the intolerable impositions placed on it by Government controls on levels of total expenditure and rate levies.

Repeated attempts to have the Secretary of State for Scotland recognize that the Western Isles is a special case have all been unsuccessful. A more generous Rate Support Grant would work some wonders, if not miracles. As it is, the authority has managed to walk a tightrope for ten years without falling off, perhaps an indication of the quality of both councillors and officials in making sure that everyone gets a slice of the annual cake; to feel a part of the island community – even if it is under a state of siege.

Comuinn Eachdraidh

In the last few years a number of communities in the Western Isles have set up Historical Societies, the Comuinn Eachdraidh. The function of these Societies is to gather historical material relating to the community, documents, records, photographs and oral recordings, and arrange these for public access. The first of these Societies was set up in the Ness area of Lewis some years ago, with the aid of a Community Programme funded by the Manpower Services Commission and other bodies. The younger generation became closely involved with the project and soon gathered a great deal of material which had been left to gather dust in the attics of croft houses. Not only that, but the older generation were systematically visited and their memories were committed to tape. Recordings were made of local family history, traditions, songs, customs of life in bygone days, the old ways of doing things, and stories, both true and invented.

The whole exercise was an experiment in community relations, with all

The Spray *fishing for lobster off Barra* (over)

An Education Committee meeting of the Western Isles Council, Stornoway. Education makes up the biggest slice of expenditure in the Council's budget

ages taking no little pride in the eventual display of the history of the area in annual exhibitions. The success of the Ness Historical Project was taken up by other areas throughout the Western Isles and, at the present time, there are a dozen or so historical societies whose members devote time and energy to preserving their past. An important ingredient in this work is the involvement of children, whose formal school education rarely allows a local dimension to be included in the curriculum. In Barra, for instance, children, through directed school projects, have uncovered material relating to the island's fishing industry, including letters, documents and artefacts. Through these projects the island children now have a direct and tangible link with the past years of their parents and forebears, giving them a valuable identity of association with their island.

Some societies have reached the stage where their efforts are now in published book form: both Tong and Tolsta in Lewis have achieved this. Other societies are busy converting old mills, such as at Dell in Lewis, to working museums, taking over old buildings, such as disused school-

138

houses, to provide a focal point for locals and visitors alike to see and appreciate the development of a township area. In Northton, Harris, a house is being converted into a genealogical facility, where information about the islands' families will be freely available and easily accessed, and where the consuming interest in 'Who were we?' and 'Where did we come from?' can be satisfied.

Uncovering the past has been given recognition by the Local Authority in its establishing a Western Isles Museum Service, looked after by a Curator. Part of the old Town Hall in Stornoway now houses Museum nan Eilean, containing a display of items of great interest relating to Lewis and Stornoway. When one considers the large number of finds and items of local interest which have gone out of the island over many years, and which now adorn the display cases of other museums in Edinburgh and London, such a facility was long overdue.

7. The language of Eden

If the landscape of the Western Isles can be said to be a museum, then the folk of the Western Isles are also living depositories of what was once the glory of Scotland: the Gaelic language and its culture. Gaelic is spoken by around 90 per cent of the Hebridean population, with even higher concentrations in certain areas and islands. A bilingual policy, promoted by Comhairle nan Eilean, the Western Isles Islands Council, since 1975, attempts to give Gaelic equal validity with English which, of course, is spoken by all native Gaelic speakers. At the turn of the century literally thousands spoke Gaelic only in Scotland, among a total of some 250,000. Today the Censal Returns show that the number of Gaelic speakers has declined to about 80,000.

Like so many minority languages, Gaelic has had a history of struggle to survive against many acts of repression, suppression and activities which were tantamount to genocide. Unlike Welsh, a sister Celtic language, Gaelic has not achieved the status of being recognized by the State. Because of that, all the kudos, in cash and kind, which helps to strengthen the role of Welsh in Wales has been denied to Gaelic. Only in recent years have moves been made to mount a strong revival of the language, with limited financial support from Government sources. What is being done today, and what has been achieved in the last decade or so, is the result of individual efforts.

Gaelic is a member of the Celtic group of languages; they in turn are a branch of the Indo-European family of languages. Thus Gaelic is cousin to Latin, English, Russian and Urdu. The present-day Celtic languages are Scots, Irish, Manx, Gaelic, Welsh, Breton and Cornish, though the latter had died out and has since been revived. Other Celtic languages once existed in Europe, such as Gaulish in what is now France, but are now long since extinct. These tongues spread far and wide over Europe some two thousand years ago and now exist only in placenames and loanwords.

There is no indication of the time when Gaelic arrived in Scotland from Ireland but it is accepted that by the fifth century AD there was a considerable Gaelic-speaking settlement in the area known as Dalriada: present-day Argyll.

There was in Scotland, however, another Celtic language, related to

Welsh, which ran through the Pictish territories of what is now Strathclyde and the Edinburgh-Forth regions. There is some evidence that the language of the Picts had some Gaelic elements, no doubt derived from their trading connections with the north of Ireland. Again, from the evidence of the placenames, there was a considerable overlap between Pictish and Gaelic, particularly in the west of Scotland.

Once the Scotii, or Irish, had entrenched themselves in Dalriada, their tentacles spread throughout Scotland – taking Gaelic with them – to establish new power bases. The spread of Gaelic was also aided in no small way by the arrival of St Columba in Iona in 563.

The movement throughout Scotland of the Columban churchmen was an important factor which increased the linguistic dominance of Gaelic in Pictland. Indeed, the gradual adoption of Gaelic as a lingua franca would have stemmed from Gaelic being associated with the successful political and ecclesiastical system which existed at the time.

If the evidence of Scottish placenames is considered, along with documentary evidence located in charters, State papers and chronicles, it is clear that Gaelic speech, and persons of Gaelic nomenclature, are to be found in virtually all parts of Scotland, with the Lothian (Edinburgh) region least affected then as it is today. There was even an infiltration into the regions south of the Border in the tenth and eleventh century, when Gaelic names of places appear in documents, though this was shortlived.

By the eleventh century Gaelic had its maximum spread over Scotland, with Welsh (as spoken in Lothian) and Pictish virtually extinct. An interesting incursor was, of course, Norse, brought by the Vikings who had a stay of some three centuries or so in various parts of Scotland. but while there might have been a period when the two languages existed side by side, Norse failed completely in Scotland (except for placenames) and had to be content with influencing the speech of the Northern Isles, Orkney and Shetland.

But the writing was on the wall for Gaelic. By the twelfth century the Anglian influence was increased rapidly, helped in no small way by the Anglo-Normans. As new burghs were established, Inglis or English became the language of trade and commerce. Through the influence of Queen Margaret, wife of Malcolm Canmore, English took over from Gaelic as the language of the court, the law and the church, though Latin was still to be the main medium in the latter area. Latin, in fact, has left its own legacy in Gaelic: eaglais, ministear, sagart, peann, sgriobh, leabhar, which those with a little Latin will recognize as meaning church, minister, priest, pen, write and book.

After the end of the twelfth century Gaelic started to recede from those areas in which it had previously reigned supreme as the language of the aristocracy and the governing classes. But, more importantly, it was being replaced by Inglis, later to be known as Lallans or Scots, as the language of the common folk. Thus over the ensuing centuries the geography of its

Gaelic drama. The Point Players won several prizes at the 1986 MOD in Edinburgh with the play Oidhche na Seachd Sian. *The company and writer all come from Lewis*

domain resembled balding patches until, by the eighteenth century, its use was confined to the west and north-west of Scotland and the Inner and Outer Hebrides. However, it did linger on in some areas in Scotland. It survived in odd pockets in the south of Scotland through the seventeenth century, along with the common Scots which had been its companion for at least a century before. It disappeared from Fife in the sixteenth century, but survived until last century in parts of Aberdeenshire and even in Upper Deeside until the 1950s. As a native language it was spoken 20 miles from Glasgow within living memory. Today, the main Gaelic-speaking domains are west Inverness-shire, West Ross-shire and, in particular, the Western Isles.

This brief account of the rise and decline of Gaelic in Scotland does not, however, highlight the punitive measures taken against the language.

Linguistic repression started with the Reformation in Scotland, a time when the Protestant religion was in the ascendancy. Religious zealots harried and burnt monasteries, abbeys and cathedrals, to leave the many sad ruins of once magnificent buildings which can be seen throughout Scotland today. Only the Highlands and Islands managed to escape much of this harrassment and held firm to the Catholic faith.

But, even before the Reformation, the Scots Parliament and the royal court in Edinburgh tried to reduce the Gaelic-based influence of the Highland clans, mainly for political reasons. The main target was the Lordship of the Isles, a Gaelic-speaking political confederacy which was strong enough politically to arrange treaties with England. To have such a strong political barb in the side of the Scottish throne was unbearable. In 1609 the Statutes of Iona were promulgated in which the power of the clans were reduced, the Lordship of the Isles having been emasculated by the 1490s. These Statutes forbade clan chiefs from maintaining their tais of armed men and, more particularly, those of their households who were keepers of Gaelic culture: bards, pipers, harpists and sennachies (story-tellers and keepers of the chief's genealogy). These Statutes were similar to those of Kilkenny, 1367, which acted against the Irish language in the same way. Only Henry VIII's Act of Union in 1536, which gave special attention to the Welsh language, saved that language from the kind of cruel attention which Irish and Gaelic received in later centuries.

The early decision by Presbyterian educationalists to adopt English as the most suitable language for teaching the Scriptures was a major disaster for Gaelic, and became the source of a language problem which dogged Highland education well into the nineteenth century. The Church of Scotland laid the foundations for a tradition of Gaelic worship, but this was done largely through a fear of a Counter-Reformation in the Highlands. And, because of her long-term policy of anglicization, the Church refused to make any further use of Gaelic in the newly-settled schools.

Even so, some credit is due to the Church of Scotland for the production of religious works in Gaelic, from which the language emerged from its deeply-entrenched oral tradition to the status of a literary medium. However, the original tolerance towards Gaelic melted, as reflected in a statement of the Synod of Argyll in the seventeenth century: '... the knowledge of the English language is so necessary for the weall of the Gospel'.

In 1701 the Society in Scotland for the Propagation of Christian Knowledge (SSPCK) was founded. Its role was two-faced. Despite the provision of the Catechism and Metrical Psalms in Gaelic, its school-masters were reprimanded for teaching Gaelic-speaking children to read those books. In fact it was Dr Samuel Johnson, no great lover of the Scots, who was instrumental in bringing before the general public the fact that the SSPCK was actively preventing a translation of the Bible into Gaelic from being published. He wrote: '. . . there remains only their language and their poverty. Their language is attacked on every side. Schools are erected in which English only is taught and there were lately some who thought it reasonable to refuse them a version of the Holy Scriptures, that they might have no monument in their mother tongue'. The good Doctor's companion, James Boswell, thought this letter of 1766 to be the finest work from Johnson's pen.

Then came the period known as the Highland Clearances, which lasted effectively for nearly a century and a half, during which native folk were cleared off their land. The reasons for this sad phase in Highland history are many and varied, but were essentially because former estates owned by clan chiefs were sold to the wealthy barons of the Industrial Revolution, who cared little for the people who depended on the land for their subsistence. The introduction of sheep required vast empty expanses of land: people interfered with the profits these animals made and so were forcibly removed from their homes. The removal of whole swathes of the Highland and Island population, bound together by language, was an act bordering on genocide. In terms of the Gaelic speech community, the Clearances period could be regarded as the removal of a linguistic heartland. It totally changed the linguistic geography of Scotland and reduced the Gaelic-speaking areas to the fringes of northern and western coastal areas and the Western Isles. Thus, commerce, religious agencies and, indeed, Governments have contributed hugely to the decline of Gaelic.

Then came the teaching out of Gaelic, by means of the 1872 Education Act, in the text of which Gaelic and its culture was completely ignored as a matter of State education policy. Gaelic had to wait until 1918, when it was given a reluctant mention in the Education Act of that year. Even so, though Gaelic was allowed by law to play some kind of role in the education system of Highland children, teachers were unwilling to use the language. There are people living today who remember being caned by the headmaster because he had heard them using Gaelic in the school playground.

Faced with a high wall of indifference, neglect and active opposition, it is little wonder that Gaelic declined to be used only as a language of the Highland hearth and home. Only in the last two decades, through pressure brought by individuals acting severally and in concert, has Gaelic begun to fight back.

Gaelic, however, is not merely a language; it is also the immediate manifestation of a culture, aspects of which are quite unique in Europe. In common with other Celtic languages, Gaelic culture straddles across some two thousand years – and in that time has accreted mythology, folk traditions, poetry and, of great importance, folktales, some of which have been accorded an international ranking by experts in this particulr field. Much of the extant corpus of Gaelic culture has been transmitted orally

Gaelic-language school, Breasclete, Lewis

from generation to generation for centuries, held in the fantastic memories of folk who were illiterate in their own language, yet who could recite the great Gaelic stories without hesitation.

When the pioneer folktale collector, John Francis Campbell – a native of Islay in the Inner Hebrides – began collecting around 1860 he discovered, especially in the Western Isles, old men and women who were the hereditary keepers of a remarkable wealth of oral tradition. Some folktales took days to recite. One, published by Campbell, runs to some 40,000 words, the length of a shortish novel. But Campbell did much more than merely collect Gaelic material. He drew the attention of scholars and a general public, at a time when 'folklore' was beginning to assume the status of an anthropological science, to the existence of an important body of tradition that might otherwise have continued to be neglected and, indeed, might well have been lost entirely. The work of Campbell and his collecting helpers inspired others to continue in the field. Their activities also gave a fresh accession of prestige to storytellers

Simultaneous translation of Gaelic into English at an Education Committee meeting, Western Isles Council, Stornoway

in Gaelic communities and there is little doubt that some stories which can still be recorded today would not have survived in oral form, had they not been coaxed out of the memory of some old storyteller in the presence of a younger audience.

Campbell found the Western Isles a living depository of a mass of oral tradition. As he wrote: 'The next step was to spend a summer holiday in studying the actual condition of this popular lore, where I had found it existed in the greatest profusion. I landed at Lochmaddy, in North Uist, and walked with a knapsack to the Sound of Barra, and back to Stornoway; crossing the Sound of Harris in a fishing boat. I found a population differing from that of the mainland, perhaps the least changed from their old ways of any people in the kingdom . . . Men and women of all ages could and did tell me stories, children of all sizes listened to them; and it was self-evident that people generally knew and enjoyed them. Elsewhere I had been told that, thirty or forty years ago, men used to congregate and tell stories; here, I was told that they now spend whole winter nights about the fire listening to these old world tales.'

Campbell gives a description of a typical storyteller, one of the finest he encountered in the Western Isles: Donald MacPhee, who lived at Carnan an Iochdair, at the north end of South Uist. The ruins of MacPhee's house can still be seen; the last occupant, a descendant of his, emigrated to Canada with his family in the 1920s:

> Let me describe one of the old story men as a type of his kind. I trust he will not be offended, for he was very polite to me. His name is MacPhee; he lives at the north end of South Uist, where the road ends at a sound, which has to be forded at the ebb to get to Benbecula ... He told me nine stories and, like all the others, declared that there was no man in the islands who knew them so well. He could not say how many he knew. He seemed to know versions of nearly everything I had got; and he told me plainly that my versions were good for nothing. 'Huch! Thou hast not got them right at all.' They came into his mind, he said, sometimes at night when he could not sleep – old tales that he had not heard for threescore years.
>
> He had the manner of a practised narrator, and it is quite evident that he is one; he chuckled at the interesting parts, and laid his withered finger on my knee as he gave out the terrible bits with due solemnity ... The light came streaming down the chimney, and through a single pane of glass, lighting a tract in the mist of the peat smoke, and fell on the white hair and brown withered face of the old man, as he sat on a low stool with his feet to the fire; and the rest of the dwelling, with all its plenishing of boxes and box-beds, dishes and dresser and gear of all sorts faded away through shades of deepening brown, to the black darkness of the smoked roof and the peat corner.

Of other performers, Campbell wrote: 'One man is a peasant historian and tells of the battles of the clans; another, a walking peerage, who knows the descent of most of the families in Scotland, and all about his neighbours and their origin; others are romancers, and tell about the giants; others are moralists, and prefer the sagacious prose tales, which have a meaning and might have a moral; a few know the history of the Feni, and are antiquarians. But though each prefers his own subject, the best Highland storytellers know specimens of all kinds. Start them, and it seems as if they would never stop. I timed one, and he spoke for an hour without pause or hesitation, or verbal repetition.'

Running parallel with the oral tradition was that of the bards, whose poetry was occasionally written down but, by and large, was committed to memory and so transmitted by frequent recitation from one generation to another. In Celtic society the bard occupied a place of honour – as did the 'filli', who were poets and musicians of higher grade than the bards. They were often attached to the royal courts of kings and, in later times, formed an essential part of the households of clan chiefs. They were to be included among those of the chief's retinue proscribed by the 1609 Statutes of Iona in an attempt to diffuse the hitherto strong position of these hereditary

keepers of clan history, genealogy and traditions. So highly esteemed was the profession of bard that even those most distinguished in social rank were proud to be enrolled in the fraternity; sometimes even those of royal lineage were to be found in it. Extraordinary honours were paid to bards and they enjoyed many important privileges. They were exempted from all tax and tribute, and were not compelled to do military service – although many actually went into battle, not so much to fight but to act as reporters and recorders, to honour the brave and the heroes and, if the battle went against the clan, to compose threnodies for the dead.

It is on record that one Highland bard, Iain Lom, stood on the battlements of Inverlochy Castle, near Fort William, marking the circumstances of the battle raging below. He was taunted by the Marquis of Montrose for avoiding participation in the conflict but replied: 'Had I mixed in the engagement, how could I have marked the many deeds of valour so nobly achieved and, had I fallen, who would have sung your praise?'

One of the most outstanding of bardic families is that of the MacMhuirichs, who gave to Gaelic poetry a length of service which amounts to well over 500 years. The family's origins were Irish and, effectively, they emerged in the early part of the thirteenth century. Thereafter, succeeding generations found themselves with patrons who were closely associated with the sources of power in the Gaelic dominium of the Lords of the Isles. Latterly, their connections were with the Clanranalds who held, among other territories, lands in the Uists. All members of this family were professional genealogists as well as poets; they kept historical and genealogical records and were thus important tradition-bearers. When the family eventually went to reside in South Uist, at Stilligarry, they were given lands to be held in return for the keeping of a record of the genealogy and history of the MacDonalds of Clanranald. They were obliged to pass on instruction in these subjects to their heirs: to a son if they had one, or to a brother's son, or to some more distant heir. The last professional member of the family, Lachlan MacMhuirich, stated in 1800 that he could not write and he put finis to an amazing dynasty which stretched from the early thirteenth century to the mid-eighteenth century and, if the Canadian branch can be included, to the early twentieth century.

Among other aspects of Gaelic culture is its musical tradition. The Gaelic-speaking Western Isles are the richest storehouse of traditional folksong in Western Europe with, in particular, one form which survives in these islands and nowhere else: the waulking song. These are labour songs sung during the hand-fulling, or thickening, of home-woven cloth, now usually known as Harris Tweed. The songs are, of course, part of a larger corpus of what are called working songs: tunes sung during

Murdo MacFarlane, Melbost bard

Ruaidhidh MacThomais, or Derek Thomson, Gaelic poet

domestic activities such as milking, herding, spinning and weaving to lighten the drudgery of the work. Other types of songs in the Gaelic traditional repertoire include rowing songs and walking songs.

The waulking process involves a group of women, half on either side of a long table, with one woman overseeing the proceedings. The cloth is first well-soaked and, as it is pulled and pushed along the length of the table, it is thumped and generally thoroughly worked with the hands. All this is done to a rhythm which easily generates the beat for singing. The woman in charge sings a verse and the group join in a chorus. The words of the songs include ballads, recitations of amorous adventures of local lads, and satirical verses. But the texts of some of the songs go back in time as far as the sixteenth and seventeenth century. The following description of waulking is from an account written by the late Annie Johnston, of Barra, a gifted woman who had an intimate knowledge of the Gaelic oral tradition of her native island. The translation from Gaelic is by Dr John Lorne Campbell of Canna, who has done sterling work in the field of Gaelic studies and who, over the years, has published the songs and words of a unique collection of waulking songs gathered by Donald Mac-Cormick of Kilphedar, in South Uist:

> When the web of cloth came home from the loom, they used to decide which night they would have for the waulking. There was the food to be prepared, fresh butter, oatcakes and barley cakes to be made, whisky to be brought home, crowdie and gruthim (a mixture of butter and crowdie) to be made, a hen or two to be killed and prepared, and then word would be sent to the waulking women. There would be a host, and the waulking-board would be in his care. This was usually made of wooden planks put together, or else, if they had one, a door would do.
>
> The number of waulking women was according to the size of the cloth and, if it was blue cloth, there had to be two teams, working in turn, to make it really tight. Usually five or six was the number that could sit on each side of the waulking-board. The women used to come, wearing calico petticoats, drugget coats and tibbet aprons. Then the hostess used to baptize the cloth, that is, she shook holy water on it in the name of the Trinity, and put it in a tub of urine. They used to say that nothing was so good for taking the oil out [of the cloth] as urine. They used to take the cloth out of the tub and put it on the board, as you saw, and doubled it on the board thus. Then the woman who was best at singing began with a slow song, and then a 'warming-up song', and after that a short light song to encourage them because they were getting tired.
>
> After this the hostess would measure the cloth with her middle finger, and usually there was not much shrinking in it at the first three songs. Then another one would begin; she would sing three songs too and, as the cloth had been warmed by the first three songs it would shrink more at the second attempt, and at the third attempt it ought to be ready, if it were a blanket or white cloth.
>
> At first it was eight finger lengths (ells) broad. When the cloth was ready it would be three inches narrower in breadth anyway.
>
> If it were blue cloth, that is, the cloth the men wore on board the boats, it would be made much thicker, and another band of waulkers would need to go to the board when the first band was tired.
>
> When the cloth was as thick as was desired, the women then used to put it on

Barra airport. The vast cockle-shell beach joining the island's northern promontory is surely the only airport in the British Isles where flights must be timed to coincide with the ebbing tide (over)

the coinneal, that is, rolling it up in a roll, and singing an oran basaidh, 'clapping song'. Clapping songs were usually light and funny, such as:

'Who will I take with me on the Irish ship?' or, 'Ho, my sweetheart, he my sweetheart' and so on.

I never heard them have a blessing in Barra, though I asked many people about it; but one of the waulking women would say to the host, if the cloth were for him, 'Enjoy and use it, pay the dance, and throw across the next web'. If it were for a young man, 'Enjoy and use it, tear and rend it, and marry before it wears out'.

Then the waulking women used to wash themselves, and come in for food and a dram, and the young men used to put the waulking-board out into the barn, and the young folk would collect for a dance.

These occasions were important socially, integrating all members of the community into a tight unit, and afforded the opportunity for the younger members to be exposed to the rich traditional heritage of their race. But the waulking was not the only time communities got together. The long winter nights were often shortened by gatherings called ceilidhs, where stories were told, songs sung and the local bard was given the opportunity to record the communities' events in verse, or else gave vent to popular feeling with scurrilous verses on, say, a local landowner or his tractor.

There are two stories about how the Western Isles came into being. One concerned a giant with nine heads who regularly demanded his favourite food: young girls. After suffering his demands for so long the people determined to kill him. One young man volunteered and, like David with Goliath, managed to put an end to the giant. The problem then was how to bury him, for there was no piece of land big enough for a grave. So they heaved the body into the sea. There the body gradually disintegrated to leave all kinds of flotsam and jetsam, with the bones turning to rocks and cliffs to eventually form the chain of the Long Island. The giant's several heads, which had been cut off and also thrown into the sea, became the islands of Eriskay, Berneray, Mingulay, Vallay, Grimsay, Taransay, Pabbay and Killegray.

The other story concerns a Viking pirate who paid regular visits to the Western Isles, then one long island, to plunder. Year after year he came, facing the stormy waters of the Pentland Firth which separates the Northern Isles from mainland Scotland. Then, one year, it occurred to him that if he towed the island nearer home he could continue with his raids but with less inconvenience to himself. So he asked a passing mermaid what material would make the strongest rope. She replied the hair of many maidens, untouched by iron. So he went to the Long Island, captured as many young women as he could and offered them their freedom if they would cut off their hair and make him a rope. All agreed, but one cursed her hair before giving it to the Viking. In due time, the rope was made and fastened between his longship and an archway at the Butt of

Lewis, part of which can still be seen today. Then, as the wind filled his sails, he tugged at the Long Island. Slowly but surely the island began to move until that same wind caught in the hills and created a fearful turbulence. At that, bits of the Long Island began to break away. Barra broke off from South Uist. That then parted from Benbecula, and so on until Lewis only was left but still clinging by an isthmus to Harris. Then that part of the rope made from the cursed hair broke completely and the Viking was left with his ship sailing away from receding Lewis.

Many of the stories told in the ceilidh house in the Western Isles are common to those found all over the Highlands. They include tales of the Each Uisge, the water horse, which could assume the form of a handsome young man, searching the sheilings for the girls who looked after the cattle on the summer pastures far away from the village. They take in fairy changelings – when a human child is stolen from a cradle and replaced by an aged fairy man – and stories as to how birds, animals and fish got their names. The haddock, for instance, still shows the marks of St Peter's fingers as he picked up that fish from the sea.

Much of the folklore of the Western Isles is contained in a massive six-volume collection, gathered by Alexander Carmichael in the latter years of last century, and published under the title *Carmina Gadelica*. There are tales of spirits battling in the skies, with their blood dropping to earth and drying on the rocks. Which is why rock lichen, when gathered and used for dyeing wool, turns the wool a dark reddish brown. There are eerie tales of ghosts of the dead and of wraiths, or ghosts of the living. Indeed, there is a magnificent rich store of material, all of which reflects the past life of the islefolk. Though little of this material is nowadays related, it has much of it been recorded and, therefore, has been saved for posterity.

One peculiar feature of the placenames of the Western Isles is the mixture of Norse and Gaelic. Most named settlements tend to be of Norse origin, while the topographical features, such as hills, have retained their Gaelic names. Callanish is a peninsula made up of round hills and vales and derived from *kollr* (a round hill) and *nes* (a promontory). Back, in Lewis, is from *bakki*, an elevated stretch of land. Ben More, on South Uist, once bore a Scandinavian name, Keitval, while Hecla, a little to the north, still retains its Norse origin. Stornoway is derived from the Norse for Steering Bay.

Most of these names tell something of the unwritten history of the Western Isles during the Norse occupation, which lasted some four centuries. As invaders, they were daring mariners who lived along the coasts of Norway, Sweden and Denmark. They sailed in open boats across dangerous waters and with their warrior skills subdued the islesfolk into accepting their authority. Establishing powerful settlements, the Norse governed the Western Isles, as they did all the west coast of Scotland down as far as the Isle of Man. Indeed, a little-known fact is that, according to an ancient law, Lewis can claim a seat in the Tingwall, the

Parliament of that island. Lewis became a dependency of Norway and was governed by a long succession of feudal kings until the dominance of that country was shattered at the Battle of Largs in 1263.

As to the name, Lewis, it is reckoned by some that the name was called by its natives Leuthas (the 't' vowelised by the aspiring h) and in imitation of this name the Norse adopted Ljodhus, after a once powerful and fortified city, Liodhus, in the south of Sweden. This town still survives today under the name Lodose. Why Stornoway, the capital of the Western Isles, has never 'twinned' itself to Lodose is a question which must remain unanswered. Yet, such a twinning would re-establish a connection which is more than one thousand years old.

The language spoken in the islands at the time of the Norse hegemony was Irish Gaelic, which was the language of the kingdom of Dalriada and the Inner Hebrides. One might have thought that Norse would have dominated completely, but this was not the case. After the Norse presence failed, Gaelic took over once more – but not before Gaelic had absorbed many Scandinavian words; no fewer than 500 words are actually common to Gaelic and Old Norse. As for the Norse placenames, while their origins remained Norse, they gave way to Gaelic inflection and eventually modern Gaelic names.

As for the islesfolk, they still have in them the roving spirit of the old Vikings, for they can be found in all quarters of the globe. The sea is still the age-long road away from the islands; but it is also the road back to the native heath, hearth and home.

The present position of Gaelic in the Western Isles is one of a slow recovery from its neglected past. When local government in Scotland was reorganized in 1975, the islands were combined into one Authority, Comhairle nan Eilean, which immediately adopted a bilingual policy. This policy has endeavoured to promote the extended use of Gaelic in many areas of public service, and particularly those in which Council employees come into direct contact with the general population. In addition to the Council's own efforts, a number of projects were established, with funding from various private and Government sources, to devise methods by which Gaelic could be integrated into the school curriculum in primary schools throughout the Western Isles. The result has been that, in general, children are encouraged to use Gaelic in their school life and be more confident in their use of it in their homes.

The public exposure of Gaelic is seen throughout the islands in street names, names on public buildings and in road signs. Gaelic also appears in the columns of the two main newspapers which circulate in the area: the *Stornoway Gazette* and the *West Highland Free Press*. These appearances cater for those native Gaelic speakers who are also literate in the language, which is not often the case. Many, particularly those of an older generation, are fully articulate in the spoken medium but find difficulty with the written word, especially when it appears in the forms of modern

Fiddle class, Barra Festival

Gaelic usage. Many, however, are more than familiar with the Gaelic Bible which they read with consumate ease, the language of the translation being more akin to that which was spoken a few decades ago. The same, however, cannot be said with English. Readers may well be able to cope with the journalese English of the tabloids but may not be so *au fait* with the more standard English of the quality newspapers.

One major boost to the presence of Gaelic in the islands was the setting up of Radio nan Eilean in 1979. News and other programmes are broadcast almost wholly in Gaelic and its daily appearance on the air waves is an undoubted cohesive element within the community since it offers, among other things, a contemporary model for the language. Most of the island communities are Gaelic-speaking, though English is used often enough. Benbecula reflects the existence of a monoglot English-speaking population and the figures for native Gaelic speakers, relative to the total population, is lower than elsewhere in the Western Isles, which is to be expected. Some communities are identified as being as much as 98 per cent Gaelic-speaking. Stornoway, being a kind of cosmopolitan community, puts a brave face on its own showing, around the 70 per cent mark.

Two important annual events are based on Gaelic culture. Feis Bharraidh is held in July of each year in Barra, as a festival of music, and has proved to be a major attraction for visitors who indulge in piping, dancing, singing and the music of the Highland harp, the clarsach. Visiting tutors are employed to teach various skills, to the extent that there is now a flourishing musical fraternity in the southern Isles. The other Feis is a three-day festival held in Stornoway in November of each year, through which a range of activities ranging from concerts, drama, exhibitions and traditional Gaelic music is presented. Both these festivals are native-born and are significant in that they present a 'live' face to counter much of the 'canned' culture which is available on radio.

One very heartening trend is the increase in the number of people who opt to learn Gaelic. Many incomers to the islands find that they become better integrated with other members of the community if they proffer a linguistic hand of friendship, which is readily taken up by the native islesfolk. Many learners have reached the stage where they have become quite fluent in Gaelic.

In 1986 a small schoolroom in Breascleit, on the west side of Lewis, became the focus of attention, for its pupils are being taught through the medium of Gaelic. If this innovative experiment succeeds, other primary pupils will be exposed to this more functional use of the language.

One last point has to be made. If readers wonder about the heading of this chapter, it was once held in tradition that Gaelic was so old that it was the language of Eden. Far-fetched, perhaps. But when one considers the actual linguistic parentage of Gaelic, the legend may not be so far from the truth!

Dance class, Barra Festival

8. Outside looking in

The realization that another kind of world existed in the remote islands of the Hebrides came to the British public rather slowly. Occasionally they might read in newspapers, chapbooks and similar ephemera about such events as the massacre of Glencoe in 1692, Jacobite Highlanders in revolt against the Hanoverian succession, Dr Samuel Johnson's Highland jaunt, or even the unprecedented marriage of Queen Victoria's daughter Princess Louise to the young and handsome Marquis of Lorne, the very first time royalty married itself to a slightly lower echelon of British society, and a Highlander at that.

Only when ships began to ply the waters off the west coast of Scotland did tourists put the Western Isles on their itinerary and then they feared the worst. What would the people be like? How could they communicate with monoglot Gaelic speakers? Would the accommodation be primitive? Indeed, with so much of the seas round the Hebrides being, as yet, uncharted, was there the danger of shipwreck? All these and other questions were, no doubt, asked as they applied for a passage to take them to the Western Isles. And they would have been asked with no little hint of excitement, for such a visit was tantamount to going on safari to the dark and unknown places of unmapped Africa. What these intrepid tourists found at times delighted them, at times amazed them, and their reports, both private and published, have fortunately given us in the present a fascinating glimpse into the past. They show the folk of the islands struggling under great difficulties with poor housing, little medical facilities, few if any roads and the lack of necessary financial resources to exploit, develop and improve their social conditions.

These reports are interesting because they show the sharp contrast between conditions in the Western Isles then and now. They are often harrowing; for instance, when describing the methods used to force people on to the emigrant ships. In these days when the conservation of wild life is accepted as 'the right thing to do', it is often appalling to read of sportsmen using the Hebrides as a free-for-all shooting range, killing everything in sight. Yet there are occasional glimpses of the world of the islanders, in which the folk made the best of the conditions in which they

Ardvourlie, Harris

A tourist examines the Callanish megaliths, Lewis

lived, kept alive a magnificent Gaelic cultural tradition, and carved out for themselves and their children a future which maintained the highly committed and independent population which exists today.

Few, if any, of these tourists of last century and the early decades of this century had any direct association with the islands. Thus, lacking the modifying knowledge of history, their reports tend to be prejudiced, comparing their own civilized lives with what they found in the islands. But some managed to penetrate the obvious to ponder the social conditions in which the islanders lived: like Mrs Frances Murray who survived a shipwreck in 1882. Relating her adventures to the members of her local Church of Scotland Literary and Scientific Society, she said of the crofters that they were 'kind, gentle, courteous and very hospitable. It was indeed touching to receive, out of their poverty, presents of milk, eggs and potatoes, though sometimes the milk or bottle of cream tasted so of peat that we could hardly make it palatable.' Mrs Murray ended her talk by saying:

In the meantime, let what of the land can be given, be given to the crofters, and that not the worst but the best, putting townships before sheep farmers wherever this can be done. These are some of the means to win back to loyalty a strong, generous and splendid race, which has filled our armies with recruits of the best kind and our families with valuable servants.

The years 1835 and 1836 were burnt into the memory of the Barra community. The weather was so bad that potato and corn crops failed and the fishing yielded such poor results that it was hardly worth the effort to go to sea. The result was, not only on Barra but throughout the west coast of Scotland, that the people faced the spectre of starvation. An appeal was launched which reached £50,000, enough at least to alleviate suffering. Two men who were responsible for administering the fund visited Barra and recorded what they encountered; they were justly appalled at the conditions in which the islanders were forced to live:

> The hut frequently, or rather generally, consists of a butt and a ben – one end is occupied by the family and the other by the little cow, if they have one, and the pig – the whole inhabitants entering by one door. The fire, which is composed of peat or turf, is in the centre of the floor and the smoke escapes by an aperture in the roof – very frequently formed by an old cask or barrel – and by the door and window, which last is seldom glazed, but is shut with straw or heather or wooden folding shutters. The roof is thatched and very warm – the floor is simply the soil, sometimes mixed with ashes and the walls, from their being in many instances formed of triturated or rounded stones and sometimes of turf, are very permeable and consequently admit a great quantity of air and moisture. But, fearful as are the physical circumstances of the people, their intellectual condition is yet more deplorable. The savage-like ignorance in which they are suffered to live and die, will not be credited by persons at a distance. It looks like a tale invented for the purpose of exciting wonder and distress, in the minds of those who have enjoyed the blessings of mental cultivation, to state that, of the 2200 inhabitants of one of the British islands, only 200 are reported as being able to read, and that, although there is a parish clergyman, as well as a Catholic priest, resident in Barra, there is no effective school in that Island or its dependencies. Yet such is the fact. A fact disgraceful to the age in which we live, and peculiarly so to those who, although connected with the islands, and themselves possessed of the blessings of education, have allowed, and are allowing, so many of their fellow creatures to pass, from the cradle to the grave, in a state of ignorance as profound as that which characterizes the New Zealander. We trust that the time is not far distant when a brighter day will dawn upon this far distant Island of the sea and the inhabitants of Barra shall, in respect to education, be placed on a footing with the most highly-favoured of their neighbours.

It is as well to point out that the housing conditions, albeit dreadful, were little better in other rural parts of the British mainland and in Europe at that particular time, and the Western Isles were often no better, nor worse, than the situation in which the peasant classes found themselves.

A visitor to Castlebay almost one hundred years later found conditions

much improved, though he was hardly impressed with the village:
'Around the head of the pier are congregated a dilapidated set of wooden
huts, which forms the offices of the different fishing companies trading
here during the fishing season. Having passed between these we find
ourselves in a street with houses on one side and a dirty shore on the other.
It is neither quaint nor beautiful, but pathetically ordinary. The several
shops consist of post office, a 'sweetie shop' and several stores. One could
not truthfully describe the stores as grocer shops, when their contents
include oilskins, gully knives, newspapers and miscellaneous articles of
men's, women's, and children's wear. This variety of stock is, of course,
understandable, when one recollects that these shops serve the hundreds
of fishermen of the fishing fleet when in this port.'

One of the attractions of the Western Isles for a certain type of visitor
was the abundance of wild life, which was at one and the same time a
source of interest and sport. Victorian naturalists were a curious bunch.
They went into raptures at the sight of curlews in flight, delighted in the
graceful movement of Bewick's Swans, and marvelled at the grey seals as
they basked on the sea shore. Yet, in the twinkling of an eye, these
naturalists were transformed into predators of the worst kind. One,
Charles Peel, considered the Hebrides a paradise for the study of animals
and birds, yet thought little when he drew that same wildlife into his
gunsights. He catalogued his destructive safari in a book published in
1901, in which he also took the islanders to task for disturbing his sporting
pleasures:

> It is not conducive to sport to be followed by a gang of men and ordered out of
> the country, nor is it pleasant to be cursed in Gaelic by a crowd of irate old
> women, even if you do not understand every word they say. They accused us of
> shooting their horses and sheep, filled in the pits which we dug in the sandhills
> for geese, shouted to put up geese when we were stalking, cut up the canvas and
> broke the seats of our folding-boat, and tried in every possible way to spoil our
> sport. They were especially insolent and troublesome in Benbecula and Barra.
> Taking them as a whole, the crofters are an ignorant lot of creatures and the less
> said about them the better.

This same Charles Peel admired rabbits so much that 'in a short day we
once bagged 105 bunnies with the aid of only a couple of ferrets'. As for
the grey seals, their natural curiosity cost them dearly:

> Seals afford very good sport, for they are as difficult to stalk as red deer. I was
> once landed out of a boat upon a small island which was literally covered with
> them. By dint of much crawling on hands and knees on the hard rock (a very
> painful operation), and taking my boots off, I got an unexpectedly close shot. I
> was crawling for a lot of six when, on creeping round a rock, I suddenly became
> aware of a large eye looking sideways at me at very close quarters. I was obliged
> to fire at him, although a small one, or he would have put the others away. He
> rolled over dead and, on running up to the edge of the rock, I saw the others
> swimming about in the water, looking curiously at me. I fired my left-hand

Sea eagle re-released into the wild at Tong in Lewis

barrel at the nearest one, and he sank in about eight feet of water. Going back to the first, I measured the distance and found that it was ten feet from me when I fired at it . . . Thus I bagged my 'left' and 'right' at seals.

Another addict for field sports, only one of many who disturbed the silence of the island moorlands with the sound of gunshot, was a Captain Newall, who wrote a book with the title: *Scottish Moors and Indian Jungles*. In his way, he was a remarkable witness to human stamina and energy, though an accident in India had left him unable to walk or even stand, and he had to be carried about in an iron chair which he designed

165

Deer stalking at Eishken Estate, Park, Lewis

himself: 'With one man in the shafts, in front, and one similarly placed behind, with two, one on each side, to assist the latter, he having the principal weight, I can manage to ascend high hills, and get carried to places and over ground which would have been quite inaccessible to a pony. In fine, I shoot over dogs, and even stalk deer with success though, of course, it is shooting under difficulties.'

He rented the estate of Scaliscro, in Lewis, in 1880 and for the next four years scoured the hills and moors for game. He developed a sympathy for the crofters whom he employed as carriers and gillies. He admired their strength and prowess, no doubt being reminded of the significant contribution which Highlanders had made to the military successes of the British Empire. He stated publicly 'a great feeling of interest in, and sympathy for, this simple, brave and struggling people . . . From an Imperial point of view, any unnecessary expatriation of the islanders would be, as it has been, a national loss. These islands, Skye especially, once formed a depot from which was drawn some of the finest material in

166

the British Army. At present, in the Lews, there is a considerable number of Navy Reserve men. But, however desirable it may be to retain such valuable material for the use of the public services, the land cannot support it.

'Even if the landlords were willing to surrender their rights at the dictation of those who have no sort of sympathy with them, the congestion must be relieved ere long, and the difficulty to be faced only postponed.'

Other visitors were content to observe the Hebridean scene. One arrived in South Uist in 1872 at the time of the great fair though, for some reason, he disguised the village of Lochboisdale as 'Storport'.

The broken-down-looking inn of Storport, a one-storey edifice without 'sign' of any sort, stands at the head of a large pier or wharf, and for nine months out of ten stares with two glazed and fishy-looking eyes at the cheerless waters, broken with damp green islands, projecting reefs and floating weed. The landlord wanders away wherever business or pleasure leads him, and a dirty servant roams to and fro through rooms innocent of the taste of whiskey or the smell of smoke. But suddenly, in the spring of the year, the fishy eyes of the inn begin to sparkle and to blaze late on into the evening with a red and festive glare. The herring-fishers, like a swarm of locusts, have descended upon Loch Storport and the whole district is alive with the signs of life. The air is full of the smell of fish, the bones of boiled fish are scattered everywhere on the ground, fish are drying on the beach and on the stones above the village, the boats at the quay are full of fish newly caught – fish everywhere, and the smell of fish; tempted by which, a crowd of gulls, hundreds upon hundreds, are hovering and darting above Storport with discordant screams.

Everywhere close to the water's edge and in the water, fish, fishermen, fishing-boats, wild women, nets, ropes, and pars; a confused moving patchwork which fatigues the eye and bewilders the brain.

Through the crowd which besiege the quay walks Father Macdonald, the priest of Uribol, his white head towering over all, and his face looking at once grave, benignant, and kind. Mingled up with the crowds of strange fishermen and fisherwomen are drovers and their dogs, mendicants, shepherds out for a holiday, farm servants in gaudy finery, cattle-dealers with their pockets stuffed full of one-pound notes, and ragged cottars of the isles. Hand after hand is thrust out to grasp that of the priest; greeting after greeting is showered upon him; and many a kind word and respectful salutation is thrown after him.

Along the winding country road, as far as the eye can see, the people are coming in a thin stream; troops of cattle driven by shouting dogs, and ever breaking from the track; poor women leading their solitary cows to the market by straw-ropes; . . . tacksmen mounted on their sturdy ponies, and crofters toiling barefoot; groups of men, women, and children, gaily dressed, jolting in rude springless carts behind old horses that creep along at the pace of snails.

On the knolls above the quay, where the cattle are legion, groups of cattle-dealers and farmers are now wrangling together and bargaining at the height of their voices. The dirty inn is already crowded with drinkers, and the excitement is beginning.

Sellers and buyers have done their business, and all have now abandoned themselves to merriment . . . On a smooth bit of green above the inn a ragged bagpiper and a blind fiddler are playing different tunes, and shepherds, herd-girls, farm-women, and drovers are dancing like mad people, with the usual shrieks that accompany the Highland reel.

That description owes more to Hogarth than the reality justified, for another contemporary writer observed a more muted Uist Fair:

I doubt if any other spot could show so picturesque a cattle-fair. In the first place, all the cattle had to be brought from neighbouring isles to this common centre and, as each boat arrived, with its rich brown sails and living cargo of wild rough Highland cattle of all possible colours, the unloading was summarily accomplished by just throwing them overboard and leaving them to swim ashore.

Besides the fishers' brown-sailed boats, several tiny white-winged yachts had brought customers to the market and added to the general stir . . . Now, however, an incredible number of islanders had assembled. It seemed a fair matter for wonder where they could all have come from, but a tidier, more respectable lot of people I have never seen. These people of North Uist – now, alas! like their neighbours, so sorely oppressed by downright want – generally rank among the most prosperous of the Outer Islesmen, their patient industry being proverbial.

Naturally, there was a liberal consumption of 'the barley bree' at the market but, the consumers being all hardened vessels, no-one appeared any the worse, nor even any the livelier – and liveliness is by no means a characteristic of these gentle quiet folk, most of whom seem to be, naturally, of a somewhat melancholy temperament . . .

A whole-hearted son of the isles has just told me that I have misinterpreted his countrymen, and that the gravity is a quality of modern growth, carefully fostered by 'Free Kirk' influences. He maintains that the true nature is that which only peeps out occasionally, when the barley-bree has shaken off the acquired gravity, and encouraged the singing of rollicking songs and dancing in the energetic fashion of olden days, compared with which our most inspiriting 'Reels of Tulloch' are tame indeed.'

As the main town in the Western Isles, Stornoway had more than its share of visitors. One was James Hogg, the Ettrick Shepherd Poet, of the Scottish Borders. In 1803 he landed at Stornoway and lodged in an inn on the South Beach. Here he tried to get some sleep after his exhausting journey. But . . .

Although the island is not noted for riots, I had no very favourable specimen of their absolute command over their passions. On the very first night of my arrival a desperate affray took place in the room adjoining to that in which I slept. Several respectable men, the Collector and one of the bailiffs, were engaged in it. It was fought with great spirit and monstrous vociferation. Desperate wounds were given and received, the door was split in pieces and twice some of the party entered my chamber . . . A ship's captain in particular wrought terrible devastation. He ran foul of the table, although considerably to the windward, which he rendered a perfect wreck, sending all its precious cargo of crystal, china, etc, to the bottom and attacking his opponents with such fury and resolution that he soon laid most of them sprawling on the deck. Some of the combatants being next day confined to their beds, summonses were issued and a prosecution commenced but the parties being very nearly connected a treaty was set on foot and the preliminaries signed before I left Stornoway.

While Hogg may not have enjoyed much rest in the town, he was more than pleased with the cost of living: '. . . very good wheaten loaves, seldom beef or mutton but abundance and variety of fish, fowls, and eggs. I expected my bill to run high but I was charged no more than sixpence for each meal.'

Seventy years later, Stornoway had assumed an air of elegance:

'As a town, Stornoway is an immense improvement on Portree (in Skye). It rejoices in churches, and the shops are numerous, and abound with all sorts of useful articles. The chief streets are paved. It has here and there a gas lamp, and the proprietor of the chief hotel boasted to me that so excellent were his culinary arrangements, that actually the ladies from the yachts come and dine there. On Saturday night the shops swarmed with customers, chiefly peasant women – who put their boots on when they come into town, and took them off again and walked barefoot as soon as they had left the town behind – and ancient mariners with a very fish-like smell.'

One of the most important works ever to be published about the Highlands and Islands was the Report of the Napier Commission, appointed in 1883 by Royal Warrent to investigate the conditions of those who were, in 1886, to become crofters. The Commissioners toured throughout the region, including the Western Isles, to hear evidence given at first hand by crofters, whose ability to argue a cogent case for basic human rights often impressed them. Some of the Commissioners nearly came to grief when their ship, the *Lively*, went on the rocks just outside Stornoway, though happily no-one was lost. But that experience must have added significantly to their impressions of the social condition of the crofters, and their understanding of the urgent need to set things aright.

Though their visits to the Western Isles were functional and hardly pleasure, the Commissioners' presence produced a vast amount of factual detail about life in the islands which must be placed alongside the descriptions of those tourists who described what they found but who hardly ever bothered to understand the reasons for the parlous state of the islesfolk.

At Loch Eport, in North Uist, the commissioners were told by crofters how

repeated evictions from other districts were the cause of so many townships being overcrowded . . . Many were compelled to emigrate to the colonies, and in one ship conveying them fever broke out, to which many succumbed. Others who remained in the island got corners in other places, while the remainder were supplied with labour by the Highland Committee, until finally sent to Loch Eport, where they still struggled to exist. The hardships to which these latter were exposed between their eviction and their settlement in Loch Eport were beyond description. The houses were knocked down about their ears, and they got no compensation for anything on the ground. They got no assistance in building their new houses. It was towards the end of the year, in winter, that they were building their temporary houses.

The severities of the winter, living in rude turf huts, and without fuel, except what they had to carry twelve miles, told on the health of many. The inferiority of the soil they now lived on, and its unsuitableness for human existence, was indescribable. Notwithstanding that, they had laboured to improve it for 30 years. The crofts would not yield them as much food on an average as would support their families for two months of the year. The ground was of such a nature that it could scarcely be improved, and the soil was so much reduced by continual cropping, that it was almost useless. The place, too, was over-crowded, there being 30 crofts, on which forty families lived, where formerly there were only three.

The common pasture, if it could be called by that name, was extremely bad, so much so, that in winter those of the people who had cattle, had to keep constant watch, else they would stick in the bogs. Human beings could not travel over portions of their crofts in winter. The people were at present in poverty, and suffering privations and inconveniences of a nature to which the bulk of their countrymen were strangers. They earnestly prayed that the Commission would recommend their removal to some other place where they could live by the productions of their labours on the soil.

Inevitably, the attitudes and actions of the landowners came in for a great deal of justified criticism. With regard to the evidence given at South Uist, one of the Commissioners remarked:

There is a serious charge in the paper which requires a little explanation. It is said in reference to the emigration of the people that 'they were compelled to emigrate to America; some of them had been tied before our eyes; others hid themselves in caves and crevices for fear of being caught by authorized officers.' Did you see any of these operations?

A Yes; he heard of them, and saw them. He saw a policeman chasing a lad named Donald Smith down the road towards Askernish with the view of catching him, in order to send him aboard the emigrant ship lying at Lochboisdale, and he saw a man who lay down on his face and knees on a little island to hide himself from the policeman, who had dogs searching for him in order to get him aboard the emigrant ship. The man's name was Lauchlan M'Donald. The dogs did not find this unfortunte youth, but he was discovered all the same in a trench, and was taken off.

Q Do you really say that those people were caught and sent to America, just like an animal going to market?

A Just the same way. There was another case of a man named Angus Johnston. He had a dead child in the house, and his wife gave birth to three children, all of whom died. Notwithstanding this, he was seized, and tied on the pier at Lochboisdale, and kicked on board. The old priest interfered, and said, 'What are you doing to this man? Let him alone; it is against the law.' There were many hardships and cruelties endured in consequence of these evictions. He himself had charge of a squad of men on the road when Lachlan Chisholm and Malcolm MacLean asked him to go to Loch Eynort to bring people out of their homes to emigrate. He refused, and constables were sent for

Funeral at Dalmore, Lewis

them. The young man, Smith, he mentioned did not belong to any family going away. He was 20 years of age, and his father and mother were dead at the time. The wife of the man who was tied and put aboard afterwards went to the vessel. The four dead children would be buried by that time. These things happened in the year 1850 or 1851. The people were hiding themselves in caves and dens for fear of being sent away from the island.

He remembered seeing the people being forced into the emigrant ships at Lochboisdale by policemen and others. He saw a man named William Macpherson forced by four men to the water-side and put into the ship. Every one of the family was sent away, including the blind father. There was another case of a man named Donald M'Lellan who, with his wife and family, was taken from his house and put into a cart until they could be sent off. There were many such cases at the time. It was about 40 years ago. Seventeen hundred persons, he believed, were sent off, all of them belonging to the Gordon estate.

Sith do d'anam, is Clach air do Charn
(Peace to your soul, and a stone on your cairn)

Select bibliography

A great deal has been written over the years about the Western Isles and much of it is sadly now out of print, though no doubt a library search would reveal books about the islands. This select bibliography largely concentrates on what material is both in print and easily accessible in libraries.

ATKINSON, ROBERT; *Shillay and the Seals*; London, 1980

BUCHANAN, DONALD; *Reflections on the Isle of Barra*; London, 1953

BURNETT, RAY; *Benbecula*; Mingulay Press, Benbecula, 1986

CAMPBELL, J.L. (Ed); *Stories from South Uist*; London, 1961

CAMPBELL, J.L. and COLLINSON, F.; *Hebridean Folksongs (Three Volumes)*; Oxford, 1969 *et seq*

COOPER, DEREK; *Road to the Isles*; London, 1979

COOPER, DEREK; *The Road to Mingulay*; London, 1985

GILLIES, A; *A Hebridean in Goethe's Weimar*; Oxford, 1969

GRANT, J.S.; *Stornoway and the Lews*; Edinburgh, 1985

GRIMBLE, IAN; *Scottish Islands*; London, 1985

HARRIS TWEED ASSOCIATION; *Orain Luaidh (Waulking Songs) – Cassette Tape and Bilingual Booklet*; Inverness, 1986

HUNTER, JAMES; *The Making of the Crofting Community*; Edinburgh, 1976

MACDONALD, ANGUS; *A Lewis Album*; Stornoway, 1982

MACDONALD, DONALD; *Tales and Traditions of the Lews*; Paisley, 1967

MACDONALD, DONALD; *Lewis: A History of the Island*; Edinburgh, 1978

MACDONALD, DONALD; *The Tolsta Townships*; Tolsta Community Association, 1985

MACKENZIE, COMPTON; *My Life and Times: Octave Seven*; *(1931–38)*; London, 1968

MACLEOD, PETER; *Tong: The Story of a Lewis Village*; Tong Community Association, Stornoway, 1984

NICOLSON, NIGEL; *Lord of the Isles: Lord Leverhulme*; London, 1960

REA, F.G.; *A School on South Uist*; London, 1964

SHARKEY, JOHN; *The Road Through the Isles*; London, 1986

SHAW, MARGARET FAY; *Folksongs and Folklore of South Uist*; Oxford, 1977

THOMPSON, F.G.; *Harris Tweed: The Story of an Island Industry*; Newton Abbot, 1969

THOMPSON, F.G.; *Harris and Lewis*; Newton Abbot, 1987

THOMPSON, F.G.; *The Uists and Barra*; Newton Abbot, 1974

WITHERS, C.W.J.; *Gaelic in Scotland: The Geographical History of a Language*; Edinburgh, 1984

Index

INDEX